World Enough and Time

World Enough and Time

New and Selected Poems

Norita Dittberner-Jax

Nodin Press

Cover photo: "Park Point," John Toren
Author photo: Zoe St. Mane

ISBN: 978-1-947237-54-4

Library of Congress Control Number: 2023942351

Published by
Nodin Press, LLC
210 Edge Place
Minneapolis, MN 55418
www.nodinpress.com

Printed in U.S.A.

For my children, Eric, Jessica, and Emily.

And for Eugene, *in absentia*.

Table of Contents

Introduction | *xiii*

from What They Always Were (1995)

It Was Like This | 5
Saint Vincent's | 6
Leaving Home | 8
Halloween | 10
News Brief | 11
Tulips | 12
Portrait of Jessie at Sixteen | 13
Love Letters | 14
Theresa's Bar | 15
Cataracts | 17
Making Myself Small | 18
Sauerkraut Supper | 19
West Seventh Street | 20
Levitating Toward Duluth | 21
Poet's Corner, Westminster Abbey | 22

from The Watch (2008)

Thanksgiving | 25
January, Two Weeks In | 26
Saying Good-bye to my Daughter | 27
Regret for Things Lost | 28
Sundays | 30
Shoring Up | 31
Meditation on the Body | 32
The Vigil | 33
Landscape | 36
Ancient Rooms | 37
How To Live | 39

Lucretia | 40
Monet, Van Gogh, at Home | 41
Gargoyle | 43
Repairing the Body | 45
The Boat | 47
Einstein in San Francisco | 48
Daughter on the Mountain | 50
Birthday | 52

from **Longing For Home (2008)**

German, the Mother Tongue | 55
Longing For Home: Nurnberg | 56
Nurnberg: Diagram of a Courtroom | 57
Berlin: Kristallnacht | 58
Kathe Kollwitz | 59
Longing For Home: Warsaw | 60
Jewish Cemetery | 61
Name Tag | 62
Walking to Birkenau | 64
Postcards from Auschwitz | 65
Fever | 66
The Germans | 67
Observance | 68

from **Stopping For Breath (2014)**

Superior at the Shoreline: February | 71
Crossing the Equator | 72
Here | 73
Sightings | 74
Family Album | 75
Photo | 77
Rain | 78
My Dad Comes Back on Grand Avenue | 79

The Only Thing That Happened in 4th Grade | 80
In Memoriam | 81
Jazz Trumpeter | 82
City Trees, Coffee Shop, Spring | 84
The Catch | 85
Single | 86
Stepdog | 87
To Eugene | 88
The Tour Guide Speaks | 89
Art Museum | 90
Numbering the Oaks | 91
Pink Rose in a Slim Green Vase | 93

from **Crossing the Waters (2017)**

Hotel | 97
Going Through the Boxes | 98
Leaving the Garden | 99
Healer | 100
Madonna | 101
Retrospective: Frida in Merida | 102
Cane | 103
A Fragment | 104
Overnight Bus | 105
The Confluence | 106
Equipment | 107
The Dream of John | 108
Car | 109
The Wedding | 110
When Leaf Buds Open on the Trees | 111
Saint Francis in the Desert | 112
Sunday Morning in the Old City | 113
Family | 115
Summer | 116
Evensong | 117

from Now I Live Among Old Trees (2020)

Suitcase | 121
Appetite | 122
When Spring Came | 123
Talking to Sparrows | 124
Fast Food | 125
Horticulture | 126
Summer's Mending | 127
Tryptich: Cemetery | 128
The Eugene Letters | 130
Prosper | 134
Now I Live Among Old Trees | 136
July 4th | 137
Heating Season | 138
Talking Books | 139
Plainsong | 141
Philando Castille | 142
In Life I Was of Modest Size, In Death I Am the Garden | 143

World Enough and Time (2023)

Matins

Everything Rises and Falls | 149
High Up: Sunrise | 150
The Garden | 151
Pandemic Check List | 152
Easter Dinner | 153
Breaking Out: Minnehaha Falls | 154
April Birthday | 155
First Live Performance of the Saint Paul Chamber Orchestra | 156
For the Poets | 157
Relic | 158

Jesus, Hearing of the Death of John the Baptist | 159
Perspective, January | 160
Shadow | 161
Composition in Black and White | 162

The Noonday World

Lynching Memorial, Duluth, 1920 | 165
Hunger | 167
Repairs | 169
Peace House | 170
Key: A Found Poem | 172
Albeit Macht Frei | 173
Midway Airport | 174
The Coat | 176
Poem for Singles | 177
Graduate | 178

The Composition of Evening

Park Point, Duluth | 181
Yoke | 184
What I Have | 185
Ash Wednesday | 186
Motel: Note to Self | 187
Dance | 188
Cows | 189
On the Road | 190
The Life of Plants | 191
Mantle | 192
Twilight | 193

Acknowledgements | 194
About the Author | 197

Introduction

I come from music. I grew up, the sixth of seven children, going to the concerts of my siblings, choirs, music groups, quartets, trios. My younger brother, Larry, and I sat on the steps in the dark listening to my sisters and their friends singing at the piano. My father was the church soloist and my sister, a cantor at the Cathedral in Saint Paul at twenty. Larry became a musician and a composer. I, a strong alto, perhaps knew I was outgunned and took to literature and writing.

As a writer from that background, I absorbed unconsciously the flow of music, of text, how it begins, a theme, then develops, balloons out, and folds back, coming to a close, a *ritardando*. The sense of a shape. Maybe all writers have this. My family background gave me that and I recognize it for the gift it is. Praise be.

The arc of this collection covers my whole adult life. In shaping it, the concerns are often the same: family, the beloved community, which like music, develops, expands and diminishes. So much joy and loss. I've written out of a strong connection to the community and the world, finding it vibrant, but cruel and unjust as well. I've written of the comfort and beauty of the natural world. Now, as I age, the poems have a growing spiritual sense.

Let me thank the small press publishers, so committed to sustain literature—the late Bill Truesdale of New Rivers Press, Joel Van Valin of Whistling Shade Press, and, of course, Norton Stillman, the publisher of my last three collections and this new and selected collection.

Their commitment to this work over the years, their love of the word, enlarges and refreshes the community. Praise them.

from What They Always Were

1995

It Was Like This

As a young girl it was like this—
slipping out of the cabin
in early morning
down to the dock, easing
the rowboat out
onto the Apple River,
rowing, the perfect intersection
of paddle and water,
muscles pulling in waves
not waking anything, not the fish
my father would catch,
not the life in the cabin (my mother
starting the oatmeal now)
not even wanting to waken myself
from this dream of water.

Saint Vincent's

Over the portal a merciful Jesus
and the words, "Suffer
the little children to come
unto Me."
We came, tripping over our names
like untied laces,
Arlene Pulowski
Frank Hovday
Norita Dittberner

The school itself was perfectly symmetrical,
the rooms a series
of quiet assurances.
We were told that you could walk into
a Catholic church anywhere
in the world and the mass
would be the same
so we never dreamed
of the Cathedral at Chartres,
never dreamed anything
that couldn't be ordered
from Montgomery Wards.

It might have ended that way
except for the principal
Sister Frances Carmel
who lodged like a sliver in the skin
stopping us in choir
until she drew from our voices
a perfect *kyrie,*
whose hands moved in arcs of music

large enough
to encompass us.

She was the irritation,
she knew how long it takes
to make a pearl.
At dismissal she'd stand like a duchess
at the portal
and let the lines of children pass through her
like acres and acres
of shimmering wheat.

Leaving Home

As the youngest of the girls,
growing up was a trunkful of formals
my sisters wore,
high heels hard as bone.
There was a party I remember.
the mirror was polished till the peonies
could see themselves
gathered up like children.
I sat halfway up the stairs watching my sisters,
Mary Lou at the piano
pounding out Gilbert and Sullivan,
Dorothy and Janet, full-skirted, laughing.

The sisters married, each in turn,
the house emptied of them.
Abandoned as a one-eyed cat,
I slept alone above the dining room
where my mother worked her crossword puzzles
and my father tallied his books.
They must have heard
how quickly I dressed, must have seen me turn
to the stranger at the door
who smelled unmistakably
of blossom.

On the morning of my wedding,
I knelt by the buffet.
My mother held the prayerbook
with its cover of beaten wood
and together they blessed me in German.
I understood their hands on my head,

understood that I was leaving
one shore for another,
that the waters between would pass through
my own body.

Halloween

“The best ones are gone,”
the child says to her mother,
but they find one
with no soft spots
and an ample chamber for holding light.

The child carries in the pumpkin
which, like their Christmas trees,
has one bad side
flat, dirty from the ground.
“Never mind,” says the mother.

The child draws the face,
The mother carves the teeth
where the knife could so easily slip.
The sun stops playing in their yard.
“Light the candle,”
the child says.

The pumpkin leers—the knife
slipped.
The mother remembers her dead,
sees them walk crookedly
through the leaves.
Let them, she says to the child
with her eyes.
Let them.

News Brief

I read in yesterday's paper that
in the Sudan, the refugees are so weak
they can't fight off the hyenas
plucking at the bodies of their dead
relatives. I only wanted a quick
once-over to keep myself informed.
I have a bridal shower to give,
a hundred things to clean and hide.
Emergency food has been sent
to the region, but most of it is not
reaching the refugees because of
the political situation. Everyone
is coming, my sisters and cousins,
ten nieces, not counting the bride;
I've ordered the centerpiece,
tulips and hyenas. Neither officials
of the Sudan nor neighboring Ethiopia
could be reached for comment.
If the news account had been more abstract,
the shower would be perfect,
right down to the mints. As it is,
I'm planning a quieter celebration
because of the death in the family.

Tulips

My son gives me tulips for my birthday.
I arrange them
in a clear glass vase,
their thick stems rushing toward morning,
toward blossom,
Tulips at my elbow
on the table
in front of mirrors where they keep bursting
into yellow and red
into what they always were.

Portrait: Jessie at Sixteen

She arrived in a squall
of hunger,
Second child.
took my breast
in hands pink, fierce
then let it fall away
just to laugh.

I see little
of myself in her
only the hips set wide
as sentries
to guide the generations
out safely.

Where did she come from
this one who threw
her head back
at the piano
to see if she could play
the minuet blind
and how fast?

In all that Northern European blood
what was hidden from me
from her father
that she should shimmer
like a gypsy,
skirts falling in folds
of magenta, of gold,
dark eyes quickening
like castanets?

Love Letters

It is the quietest thing they've done
in years. Behind closed doors on summer
afternoons, my daughters write letters
to young men. Paper disappears
from my desk; there is a run on stamps.
Fat letters to an airman apprentice
in Pensacola, pastel envelopes
to the drummer at music camp.

Slow summer afternoons of overcast skies
and deep humidity. My daughters in their
idleness watch soap operas and file
their nails while they wait for the mail,
the pattern so set that when
my son hears from Rose in Honolulu,
after an absence of two years,
he asks for stamps.

Summer nights, my daughters fall asleep
to the strum of crickets and the whispers
of absent lovers. They waken, their faces
bright as peaches in the bowl of morning,
another day, another summer day, dozing
like cats in the sun, another promise,
write soon, write soon.

Theresa's Bar

Q: "What kind of farming do you do?"
A: "I wouldn't be farming at all, except for my son.
He died."

Three years ago now,
but for Russell
the news is fresh as spring dirt.
He so full of his son's death
the words spill over, leak out,
and I can see by his eyes
that he has been summoned again
to the field where the tractor overturned
on the boy.

You return with our beer. We talk
the three of us
about the death. Russell's face reddens
as he speaks of leaving
the farm, the memory.
Your arm is braced against the wall.
I stand in that arc, in the field
of your radiation
drawn to it out
of the cold.

All day I have moved between heat and cold.
This morning I inched my chair closer
to the fire as the day collapsed
into rain. Then when it cleared
I rode Bea through the woods,
braced my legs against her belly
and felt in her stride
the blaze of motion.

Now Russell asks me to dance.
We swing to the music of tuba,
accordion. His arms lift
to the music, "I remember the night
and the Tennessee Waltz."
He tells me which halls had
had the best dance halls before
they burned down.

When you and I dance, Russell disappears
toward the bar where Theresa
fills his glass and the crosses she wears
in her ears flash
by bar light.
We move, we don't talk.
It is a month to the eve
of our wedding. Move, love
don't talk.
We are the fire
around which terrible stories are told.

Cataracts

A smudge on the lens, dirty fingerprints
on glass. I examine my eye for outward
signs, but nothing shows. The loss is silent
and insidious as fog: the finches on the fencepost,
berries on the mountain ash, every day the list
gets longer, as I lose the particulars
of the world.

Worst of all, I lose the articulation
of shadow and light. Darkness is a mute thing
that no longer speaks to me in tongues.
On summer nights, when shadows gather in the trees,
I don't see the braid they weave. What I see
is one vast absolute.

And entering some rooms, I startle
the way an infant does, unprepared
for the abundance of light pouring in
from the windows. I shield my eyes
the way the holy women do in pictures
of the Resurrection, and turn away,
as they do, from perfect, stunning light.

Making Myself Small

For the surgery,
I make myself
very small.

My breath
comes deep and slow.

I compose my body
into a landscape
out West
where the foothills
of the Rockies begin.

I fold my toes
and cup my hands
into each other.

My whole body,
a long afternoon
with only the slightest
of winds.

I am so quiet and small
I almost disappear,

the only disturbance
the monitor bouncing
its inane ball
off my regions

from peak to peak,
the news, how I
go on.

Sauerkraut Supper

for Maryann Turner

In honor of my birthday, you ask me
to the sauerkraut supper at St. Adalbert's
in Frogtown, my old neighborhood.

We meet in the church basement, line up
with the others, large men and women
who lack confusion about who
they are, who live by rules
of beer and coffee, who drinks it,
who pours it.

We are all happy to be here,
moving in line to the kitchen
where the cook raises the lid and steam
rises like a genie.

She ladles the sauerkraut into great bowls;
other women pass us carrying platters
of roast pork, bowls of potatoes, apple pie,
a feast of pale foods.

There isn't a green for miles, no broccoli,
no zucchini, those foreigners in
the new land, nothing sharp, nothing to vex
our souls that have traveled so far
from our starched childhoods, as if

we had all pushed our chairs back
from the table and vanished, years ago,
leaving our ghostly mothers with the dishes.

West Seventh Street

This section of the city is dedicated to repairs:
Used appliances
rebuilt transmissions.
Old Fort Road begat
West Seventh. The hooves of cattle beat
this ground, this street still
has the heart muscle
of an ox.

The bus driver knows it, see
how he turns the wheel with one finger?
This is his run more
than the skyways downtown unbuttressed
by dirt.

He learned the edge of the knife here
the language of plumbers
who name their parts male and female
because one fits into
the other.

Today he watches for spring
twice uptown, twice downtown.
It squints off the bits of glass, rises
in a breeze off the river,

the river, so close, he forgets,
that before the oxen
was the river,
flicking its tongue at the land.

Levitating Toward Duluth

I watch for the first pine, a flag of the country ahead,
and listen for the knock of geography shifting gears,
land rising out of bedrock and farm field.

Everything around me appears ordinary,
but inside I am waiting to be conducted
through something grand.

We climb higher, a long string of cars
crossing the St. Louis River, cutting through
the last elevation, then on to the top.

Suddenly the lake, huge and primal,
hidden behind the hunched shoulders of the hills
and with it the ships, bridges, and railroads,

all the commerce of water and land.
For a split second, we shimmer like trout
in the great flow of it, each bay and pier,

then shoot downhill into the stone channels
of the freeway, all our climbing released,
and arrive on the other side

of the city and onto the North Shore,
quiet now, we are inside geography,
we hum along, a string of cars

whose passengers turn naturally
to the thin line between water and sky
where all our hopes gather.

Poet's Corner, Westminster Abbey

After the overstuffed chapels, the corridors
narrow with the tombs of forgotten lords,
and opening of white marble, a widening of air
that leaves room enough for thought:

> *The communication of the dead is tongued with fire*
> *beyond the language of the living.* (T.S. Eliot)

In the small library of epitaphs in stone
I read the legacy of words from which I trace
my origins, back to the overheated classrooms
in Frogtown where I first hear these voices:

> *The first condition of human goodness is something to love;*
> *the second, something to reverence.*
> (George Eliot/Mary Ann Evans)

These voices wash through me, a river
that runs underneath all the writing.
to fit the object perfectly with words,
to articulate the soul's lonely odyssey
in the world,

> *Time held me green and dying though I sang*
> *in my chains like the sea.* (Dylan Thomas)

To break silence and go back to silence,
this is the work I want to do
day after day after day.

> *With courage to endure* (The Bronte Sisters)

from The Watch

2008

Thanksgiving

They come, slamming the doors of their little cars
and bearing covered dishes, our offspring,

their spouses and roommates, all gathered
at the Thanksgiving board,

the table a pleasure, a beauty, a groan, the turkey laid out
in front of us, the handmade stuffing,

potatoes riced and creamed, the cranberries
that slid out of the can classic as Greek pillars,

ten of us, laughing, elbow to elbow, what more could I ask?
This loneliness is a way of preparing

for the next generation and remembrance of the dead.
I miss them both today.

I serve the pies, apple and pumpkin, wanting to send a piece
or two on to the other side.

Our ranks are thin, they want plumping up. This is the time
between the old and the new,

a thin layer between grief and possibility. Out of this longing
came all the generations.

January, Two Weeks In

We cannot part with it.
In early January, we slide our perfect tree outside,
bare of lights and ornaments, all the cardinals and finches,
the parrot from Brazil, the apples red with promise,
packed away.

We stand the tree smack in the middle of the front yard
where it rests in low winter light, snow softening its branches,
but in the spike of needle, from spine to spire, the memory
of wilderness.

I wish we had a whole stand of pine in our yard,
gathered like friends in time of need. But we have only this,
a fir tree, our tannenbaum, to keep the memory of forest,
of bear and deer, the earth's time,
long and steady.

Saying Good-bye to My Daughter

I wish they were neater, our good-byes.
The babies, the dog, our husbands,
all up against the door.

The best thing would be the quick
kiss, click of the seatbelt,
a final wave.

Instead we fall into each other's arms
and all the good-byes of the past
echo in the valley between us:

Baby girl, born at midnight, spirited
down the dark corridor, the first
time I missed you.

The mother and the joint custody kid
so practiced at packing;
the child who didn't want to go to school
on Monday morning.

At the front door now, with all
that clamoring to move on, we stop
to enact it all again.

Then you return to a city near water
and I re-order the house with all its light
and the shadows like draperies
I pull against the dark.

Regret for Things Lost

Not husbands or home,
not umbrellas, not the keys I've left
scattered widely as male seed
in the world,

but a shirt stolen from the clothesline
years ago, a shirt in which I felt
perfectly myself, the ache
of that blue-striped theft.

And bracelets. One from my brother
of antique silver that I wore
on my wedding day; the other
from my husband, a simple
gold band, ring for my wrist, both lost,
one in Bemidji, one in Cornwall.

Blue clip earrings, the only ones I ever loved,
sacrificed for a more severe version
of myself, the woman I was, lost,
with all her accoutrements.

There are so many things
in this culture, so many disposables,
surely there are replacements.

I wish it were enough that I remember
the blue stones
of my youth, enough
that what I put on is a flag
I'm waving to the world,

enough to be
a woman who has been given bracelets
of silver and gold,
but something in me is willful,
wanting them back,
hungry to hold them again,
my things,
jewelry in my palm,
shirt on the clothesline where I left it.

Sundays

My mother entered our house with all her good days gone,
nothing left but to live out the bad,
her whole life a streak of good luck next to this.

We pulled the wheelchair up the front steps,
and the children came to greet her,
frightened by her stillness, no relation

to the grandmother who did tip-overs with them
on the carpet. I brought in the commode, pushed it
to the corner until she needed it,

then lifted her out and sat her down.
When she finished, I gathered her up in my arms,
arranging and rearranging her garments

and returned her to the wheelchair
where she composed herself
back into the stroke.

The look we exchanged before the moment
of holding, our eyes level and straight.
Holding her longer than I needed to

(she always was good to be near),
the long moment of holding my mother,
her broken house of bones.

Shoring Up

To be with you
walking the wide
boulevards
blindingly white
in stone and shine;
to pass a café
where a waiter unfurls
a white tablecloth
like a flag saluting
the bread and wine
to come; to cross
the low bridges
of the Seine and behold!
its sheen turns
midnight blue,
the shade of the Evening
in Paris perfume
I bought my mother
at Woolworth's,
ahh, let it come,
let it all come.

Meditation on the Body

How it presents itself to the world
combed or careless, the layers
of cloth covering the smooth skin.

The body in lovemaking,
the rosy interior revealed, the desire
to be known thoroughly,
nipple and foreskin.

The body in its frailty,
arriving for surgery at an unsuitable
hour, a parking ramp orange-lit
to prevent murder, and in a cubicle
the size of your closet, removing
everything until you are down
to synapse, pulse, breath.

The body as cathedral – sanctuary,
dome, cloister –
coming full circle
from my early schooling,
the body as temple, the holy.

This body of ours,
this gorgeous flowering whose roots
pump life to every cell,
the way in
and out, a door.

The Vigil

In Memoriam Harlan Olson

1.
You come up our walk,
our best friend,
hapless with cancer.
Snow flurries drop
from an overcast sky.
We need a patch of green,
a little resurrection.
How easily we laugh in the car,
the four of us; like children
in church, covering our mouths
against the outburst of mischief,
everything hilarious.

You sit in our front yard
on the plastic Adirondack chairs
smoking a cigar. The smoke engulfs
you and then is borne away.
The limbs of the great oak
shake their fists at heaven
or reach for it.

Each time you hug me,
you hold me a moment.
I feel your bones, the timbers
of your house.

2.
When your friend is dying,
all the stoplights are red

for you. The driver in the car
turning right, the chatting couple
in the next lane, have all the time
in the world while you grip
the steering wheel white-knuckled.
You are a courteous person,
yet you give them the finger
under the dashboard. All they see
is a woman behind the wheel,
jaw line locked as a fist,
even as you realize that no
hurry of yours will change
his life, emptying faster
than you can drive.

3.

Two whole salmon with grapes for eyes,
a wheel of cheese, gallons of pasta
with tomatoes and feta – one glorious spread.

"Ninety-eight bucks for a fish!" says the man
behind me in the checkout line.
I look up and see others eyeing our order

with frank interest. The woman behind him
asks, "Having a party?" I hear myself say,
"Our best friend died."

The truth is leaking out everywhere.

He didn't get to stand in enough lines,
making good-natured talk
at the checkout counter.

His wife will be alone, as these lovers
of food are, widowed, divorced, making small
pools of community wherever they go.

Landscape

I drive across the High Bridge with St. Paul sprawling
before me, built on hills like Rome itself.

I see the cathedral piercing the sky and think
of its domed interior, its mysterious recesses

and imagine it imploding, collapsing into the nave,
and how the hills of St. Paul would go on being hills,

how everything would compose itself briefly
around the absence of the cathedral

and then just go on. This is the first time
I have accepted the idea of my own death.

Ancient Rooms

1.
I wandered into a Roman bath
and thought of the men who bathed
within its steep walls, arranging for trade
and prosperity; thought of the women
who rinsed them off from great pitchers
of water, gone, all of them gone.

I looked up at the single window and saw
the wheels of traffic on Rue Saint-Jacques
and people passing on the pavement,
their mouths moving without sound.

The sun sent shafts of light pooling into
the middle of the chamber, offering itself,
an invitation. I stepped into it,
one woman in the census of the world.

2.
A room used now for string quartets
at noon, bone-white Roman walls
around which pale medieval statues
stare, not one of them whole.

To the west, the heads of the kings
of Judah mounted on pedestals,
a chorus of judgment, mute
and terrible.

To the east and south, the saints,
some without torsos,

some without arms, even the stone
hem of a robe cut off.

What concerto could offset the white
carnage, everything human bleached out?
Afterward on the street,
I want to deny myself nothing,
live voraciously
against the time to come.

How to Live

A hundred years ago, the fire
of a Ukrainian foundry
forged this cross.

You brought it from Kiev,
the crucifix passed
from one generation
to another, the corpus
worn and shining,
a landscape of valleys
and hills and the long
geography of limbs.

It fits my hand perfectly;
my thumb worries the head,
a comfort, as it was for others
who held it in sickness
or hid it during persecution.

Sometimes now I am tired,
worn down with caring. I want
hours alone, the radio mute.

Then I wonder, which way?
Preserve myself?
Or like the little cross from Kiev,
let the blessing of hands
leave its shine upon me.

LUCRETIA

She still holds the knife
in one hand, and steadies herself
with a cord in the other.

We do not see her husband,
but he is there, powerless to protect her
from the rapist, or her own despair.

The brocade robe falls open,
framing the white chemise,
the private interior.

The wash of blood
from the wound she inflicts on herself
mirrors the other wound.

Rembrandt painted her at the end
of his life, acquainted, as he was,
with terrible loss.

How he troubled over her eyes,
more sorrowful
than any crucifixion.

Lucretia, 1666
Rembrandt van Rijn
Minneapolis Institute of Arts

Monet, Van Gogh, at Home

The wonder that Monet
had time to paint, the vast
size of the garden and across
the road, the Japanese pond,
a man enchanted with nature –
flowers, water, haystacks, and
light! A blind man's obsession
with light, every slant of the sundial
documented, time filtering
light.

What a life! Two wives
the second with six children!
No wonder the huge table
in the dining room, fourteen chairs,
all canary yellow; the blue-
and white-tiled kitchen, large
and commodious, festooned
with copper pots;
the large bedroom overlooking
the garden: to throw open
these shutters in the morning!
So much life!

Modest, difficult, van Gogh
thought himself one link in the chain
and took the yellow house at Arles,
on Place Lamartine, hoping
others would come. A table
and two chairs and just enough
left for broth and coffee.

Gauguin fled after two months
when Vincent chased him
with a razor. He painted
"Gauguin's Chair" empty except
for a lit candle, in memory
of the failure.

Toward the end, he painted
the vestibule near his room,
the yard where he was confined,
night sky from his window.

Gargoyle

For Eric

1.
Sometimes, before class, I feel shy
about being in front of them.
If I had a way out, I'd take it,
just as they would. Then I plunge
into class – they turn in late papers
and no matter what structure
I've set up, baskets, bins,
they hand them to me,
wanting an exchange of the eyes.

Sometimes in class, a student's face
changes, a slight shift of tectonic plates
exposes an angle of grief almost
unbearable.

I think, what if they all unmask,
what will I do then?

2.
I wanted light to pour in
from the windows of my classroom,
but the television is mounted there,
its cords tangled like intestine.

I wanted curves, the desks in half-
moons, but the long train
of fluorescent light burns a hole
in the dark.

What I wanted was so grand,
I forgot the postcard of the gargoyle
I taped to the podium to absorb
any misery coming my way,
saying, *Send them on up!*
Your detentions, the trouble
at home, every bridge in your life
that comes up short,

feed them to the monster, let him
chew on it while you do
the mind's work of reading
and moving your hand across paper.

3.
Their heads are bent to paper, copying out
William Blake's *The Lamb* and *The Tiger*

on opposite side of the notebooks, adjoining
poems. They will graduate in three weeks and most

I will not see again, but here, now,
we have the odd affection, the familiarity

and shyness of teacher and student, this closeness
over poems by mad William who lives on and on

becoming the gift I give these students,
and the gift they give themselves.

Be accurate, I say
and make them as beautiful as you can

and they do; the room is very quiet.
In the courtyard the lilacs open.

Repairing the Body

1.
I can stay in these four walls
with the bad news, but I can't
go into the world
without you.

2.
You take nothing with you,
your keys, your wallet, your glasses,
not even your wedding ring.
A door swings open.

3.
In the waiting room, a stranger
talks to me, but the sound is shut off.
Hands cut into the clock's face;
the sun rises.

4.
Our children, your sister, our friend
join me; you have almost as many people
as the Mexican family. The waves of English
and Spanish comfort me.

5.
I cannot stop thanking the doctor
who fixed you. The crease
in his trousers is precise, his nails,
immaculate. Praise him.

6.
Five days later, as I prepare
to take you home, the news
of Paulo's death. How ignorant
we were last month talking
with him, death hidden
like a microphone behind
the curtains, picking up
each lively word.

7.
Silence entered me this year;
I didn't rush to cover it, but let it fall.
Gradually it settled like sunlight
on our sofa.

8.
Two months since we thought
you might die, since I remembered
to dream. But now the night
holds no terror. You mend, your stitches
the railroad tracks crossing
a country I love.

9.
Lying there afterwards
I feel the perfect sense
our bodies make, and it is good,
all good.

10.
The smell of coffee, the stretch
of my body in the morning,
the old joy.

The Boat

for Monica and Bob

We slip through the darkness, feeling in the boat's rocking
the heaviness of water, under us, around us;

a halo of light in the west, the barest of moons,
the least moon possible.

Docks already gone to darkness, houses barely visible,
but the lives lived there stand in clear panes of light.

We are four friends, two marriages, taking a turn
on the lake. The wind blows up a fierce smell of water and fish.

We are quiet, surrounded by water, rocking
in the darkness of the boat, frail as moths.

Einstein in San Francisco

Post-mastectomy, you exercise to music
in the living room, while I read the Sunday paper
on the sofa, the Pacific long as the horizon
behind me. Yo Yo Ma is playing
an Appalachian lament. In my mind
I see his head bowed, his arm slowly drawing
the sweetness out of the cello.

A wild, dark energy
is pushing the universe apart.
Eventually, it will implode, a slide
into senescence.

I heard the diagnosis in a hotel room
in a strange city; the flashing of the telephone's
red light, a wild dark energy.
I came to be in the same state,
the same room with you, in the city
you've made your home,
galaxies from the high school in Frogtown
where we met.

Einstein called his theory a blunder,
but all the signs point to his genius:
the universe will cool and darken.
In 30 billion years, it will collapse
in on itself.

You're on your feet now, up against
the dining room wall, raising your arm
ten times. Wincing, brave girl.

It's no news to us that the universe
is expanding. We'll never live
in the same city again. We airlift
in and out of each other's lives
and in the long interval between flights,
we telephone our pleasure
and sorrow. There's time enough
for us to turn sixty, even seventy,
maybe eighty. Remember. Call me.

Daughter on the Mountain

Taking T'ai Chi Chih,
I'm learning
balance, shifting
my weight from one foot
to the other,
making platters, balls,
with my hands,
daughter on the mountain,
daughter in the valley.

The master tells me to keep
my mind on my feet and shift
my weight so
completely
that I could lift
one foot off
the ground.

My feet obey, but my mind
wanders back
to Jerusalem to the top
of the Old City,
the story of Mohammed,
how he rested his foot on a rock
before climbing the ladder of light,
pushing off
into the vault of the sky,
his night journey to heaven.

Rocking my body, forward
and back, I'm poised

for flight, like Mohammed.
The joy of it! How difficult
to keep my mind on my feet,
to stay in this world,
with my head full
of Mohammed and the terrible
temptation to rise.

BIRTHDAY

I drive across town, past the freeway, stoplights, each one a milestone from childhood to my old neighborhood in Frogtown. Spring has just stopped holding its breath and the soft wind barely ruffles the flag on the school. I forgot how flat the streets are, even the hill where I daringly lifted my hands from the handlebars of my bike is no hill at all. The houses are small and bony, even our house of four bedrooms seems to have shrunk. I drive past the church to the avenue the hearse took with the bodies of my mother and father, and enter their town with its low houses and tiny skyscrapers, the untrampled grass. I clean off their common stone and place the single yellow tulip between their names, *Doris, Otto,* then the long music of *Dittberner.* I stay long enough to say *thank you,* for my life, the sixth of seven children, born in my mother's 47th year, a world of ordinary houses and minimal geography, a lively mother, a singing father and a generous offering of brothers and sisters. I drive home, back across the intersections and the freeway to my neighborhood of weighty houses and hills to live out the rest of my life.

from Longing For Home

2008

German, the Mother Tongue

The sounds and shape of German
are as natural to me as a cool glass of water.

I know few words, but the sounds move in my mouth
utterly without effort, the way they tumbled

from the laughing mouths of aunts and uncles
a private code, a childhood shared, unconnected to me.

The same code my parents used with each other
while I hid under the table, trying to decipher

what they were saying in German, language of trouble,
of not in front of the children. Now, preparing for the trip,

I hear those sounds in terrible words,
musselman, kraut und ruben, Du Jude, kaput.

Longing for Home: Nurnberg

We stop for lunch and a stein of beer
and find the perfect gift
for your mother in the town square,
and all the time, we walk on sorrow
like a buried city under our feet
and under that city, another,
so many layers of that at night
every disturbance of my life
comes back to haunt me,
and I have to call home, the urgency
to connect in phone calls,
postcards, a trail back
as surely as the bread crumbs
left by Hansel and Gretel.

Nurnberg: Diagram of a Courtroom

The dignity of the room, chandeliers,
mahogany walls rubbed
to a sheen.

Twelve judges sat on the right in front of windows
whose velvet drapes were drawn
for the duration. No natural
light fell on those
proceedings.

Lawyers, interpreters, stenographers
at tables in the middle,
facing the judges.

On the left, the accused: Goring, Hess, von Ribbentrop,
Borman (*in absentia*)
nineteen others.

Near them, a brass railing and a stairway from which they entered
the courtroom and returned,
their sphere narrowed
to that vortex,
a spiraling
down.

Adam and Eve in marble over the lintel,
gatekeepers now to an empty room,
where no one comes
or goes.

Berlin: Kristallnacht

Dieser Synagogue is being restored!
It sags in the middle of the block
like a patient held up by two orderlies.

Dieser Synagogue is still in rubble
and ruin from the Night of the Broken
Glass, the beginning of the end
for the Jews in Germany.

But, work is being done, gold leaf,
fresh black paint to the ornate doors
which will open once again, the holy
place not set apart, but smack!
in the middle of everything.

Still, there will never be the throngs
there were, the old crowding,
that liveliness.

Kathe Kollwitz

> *"I do not want to go until I have faithfully*
> *made the most of my talent and cultivated*
> *the seed that was placed in me."* – *Kathe Kollwitz*

The seed planted was the eye of suffering,
mothers and children in extremity, a fist
raised in anger, a head bowed in grief,
the gnawing life of German peasants
at the turn of the century, the children
hungry, the mother's body extended,
gathering them in.

Sunlight shoots through the stairwell
as I pass between floors of her museum,
lost in her vision. Across the lawn,
I hear the bright ring of glasses,
of noon wine on creamy tablecloths,
but here, rags and despair, hundreds
of black and white lithographs, the thin
shoulders of the poor bearing up
in beautiful Berlin.

To articulate a vision this stark, this
complete. She has gone on ahead of us.
I see now how this works: the great ones
clear the field, carve out the territory.
They make maps of wilderness
which we use to find our way.

Longing for Home: Warsaw

We spend the day walking Warsaw,
so few steeples and domes,
the whole city bombed
for the uprising.

The manhole cover to the sewers
where the Jews hid is marked simply
with the number W-62.

I line up at the post office
with penniless students
wiring for money. I'm calling
home, leaving our number
in case something happens.
At home. In Warsaw.

My breath quickens
at the ringing of my daughter's phone
seven thousand miles away.
No answer.

I leave a message that fails
to register the stab of pain I feel
as I sever the connection.

Jewish Cemetery

We take the streetcar to the cemetery,
get off when we see the obelisks
behind a brick wall and barbed wire.

Everything locked. Then I notice
a dirt road leading to a lumberyard
that adjoins the cemetery –

cement mixers, piles of stone
and planks of clean lumber piled
next to the wall. I take that road,

you follow, saying we shouldn't, then
where the planks are highest, you turn
and say, "Quick, climb up and look over!"

You give me a hand, I teeter at the top
thinking what fine insurrectionists
we'd make, and look over the wall:

deep green, dense with trees, leaves
of ash and maple, the ancient gravestones,
everywhere graves, the Jews of Warsaw,

some dead for two centuries, some dead
only fifty years, but almost all of the Jews
of Warsaw dead and still behind barbed wire.

Name Tag

As instructed, she brought only one
suitcase weighing 20 kilograms
and wrote her name on it
in large block letters:
Fanny Klinger

In the mountain of suitcases behind glass
other names are visible,
Bertha Eppinghausen
Franz Engler
but the name of *Fanny Klinger*
is the one that lodges like a splinter
of bright glass in the skin.

That name sings even written
on a suitcase of brown cardboard.
Her parents must have practiced
saying it before she was born.
If the baby is a girl
we'll call her Fanny.
Fanny Klinger.
Das ist gutt.

She was someone's
childhood friend,
a shy schoolgirl, a young
woman of surprising passion
and long, dark hair.

When she packed the suitcase,
did she think with the others

that now at least the harassment
would stop? They would live
together in the labor camp,
her aunts and uncles,
her noisy cousins.

When the train stopped
and they piled out, grimy and weak,
she walked with the others
down the *Lagerstrasse.*

She saw the SS men in their spotless
uniforms toss the suitcases
in the back of a transport truck,
and ahead, the leader with a quick
glance, direct each detainee
with a flick of his index finger
left or right.

What good was her name then,
even a name as bright as a poppy
against all the apparatus of death?

Walking to Birkenau

We don't know where it is, but we're walking
the two miles from Auschwitz to Birkenau,
over the stone bridge, crossing old railroad tracks,
the way I crossed the coal yards of Frogtown.

Then suddenly, Birkenau, the long building,
the square watch tower, the arch
underneath for the train to pass through.
We stand on the tracks reconstructing
the course of that train dead ahead to inferno.

The chimneys, the fence stanchions, barbed wire
obscenities, the ruin of crematorium,
roses everywhere terrible in their frailty.
In the ash pits, poppies and clover flourish.
The sky over Birkenau is blue.

Postcards from Auschwitz

We stayed the night
in the little town of Auschwitz,
just across the river from the camp
and a few miles from Birkenau.

Our hotel was adequate and clean.
We ate an early supper in the hotel café,
then spent the evening in our room
which overlooked an open field.

Two narrow beds separated
by a dresser of poor quality
and a small table and chairs,
the only room with such a blessing.

We wrote postcards to our children.
They seemed the most important thing
we would ever send them.

Fever

On the labor crews
the prisoners were too tired
to remember, but when
sent to the infirmary
with running sores
and fever, they ached
with *Heimweh,* with longing
for home, for holy days
of prayer and fasting,
the commonest meals
with family, soup, bread,
a difficult uncle,
a Persian cat, and this
delirium was more
terrible than any labor
so they gave up and died
or returned to work
as soon as they could.

THE GERMANS

The man who found us wandering
the halls of the Palace of Justice,
looking for the courtroom and led us
to the hidden door.

Herr Grimm in Munich, financing
his own Jewish museum with the sale
of Daumier prints, giving up half
his apartment.

The woman who gave us the tour
of the Nazi stadium.

My people left. What luxury
to wonder what we would have done
had history pressed us.

Observance

What is there new to say
about the Nazis and the Jews?
Day after day I type the journals
of that pilgrimage, yoked to the task
by whatever makes writers select
their material: Nurnberg, Berlin,
Warsaw, Cracow.

Then I raise my head
from the keyboard and read the face
of the clock on the mantle:
Seven p.m., July seventh,
and July is the seventh month and seven
is a magic number, seven days
of the week, the seven gifts of the Spirit,
the seven deadly sins.

This is the exact time that we left
for Germany one year ago, me on the grant
and Gene out of his goodness
and interest. How did I remember?
Was it the heat? The Asian lilies
and the baby's breath blooming in fullness
again in the front yard?

I thought I had died from the heart up,
to do *this* work by rote,
but here it is, the living connection,
the strong desire I have to run
my hands over the cobbles of Nurnberg,
to add the name of Fanny Klinger
to those I will remember always,
the name I can never forget.

Stopping For Breath

2014

Superior at the Shoreline: February

Think of it as a kingdom of ice,
its vast depths, turbulence in check,
the beach you walked,
the red umbrella you planted
in the sand, lost.

But find a spot, dig your boots
into the snowpack. Bring the quiet
you kept while the baby
slept, that cathedral silence.
Watch the lake begin to breathe
at the seams, the slight rise and fall
of its breast, the deep push
against ice, the first crack.

It will be weeks before it gains
strength at the shoreline to blast
the rocks on which you stood as a girl,
stunned by its fierce rhythm,
in love with it, as young girls love
the galloping horse.

Crossing the Equator

I woke up
and saw the Southern sky.
We were flying a plateau
of pure color,
a heavenly blue
that cut a swath of clarity
far above weather.
On the belly of blue,
the blue of whales
and morning glories,
hung the moon,
a sliver of pure light,
its position strange,
as if some gravitational
pull had tipped it to rights,
a cap of glorious light,
ends pointing perfectly
toward earth; stars gathered
around this moon
in configurations
new to me.
I awakened to light.

HERE

I can't speak for elsewhere
but here the sun rises and sets
and sometimes you can't see it.
Gravity pulls us toward earth
which spins so slowly, you can't
feel it. Sometimes it's cold,
sometimes, hot. It sounds simple,
but the effects are dramatic –
Trees stand like bleak sculptures
for months then suddenly break
out into leaves with tiny veins
you can feel with your fingertips.
Like the nerves in the body
that power your fingers and
everything else unless you have
a stroke, an explosion in the brain.
Then you can't feel the veins of
the leaves or even sorrow you felt
last week. I can't speak for elsewhere
but here, you get used to one thing,
then it's another, like day and night,
and you want someone to answer for it.

Sightings

after Anne Carson

Rabbits on the boulevard
are a sign of God's presence.

Night terrors, the visitation
of God's angel, keeping you real.

The stubborn intractable presence
of the poor, God-with-us.

The first breath and the last,
God's portion.

Fra Angelico's "Annunciation,"
the God-particle in the artist.

God in the stance of the oak,
the surge of life upward.

In the child hiding from an embrace,
God's love coming forward.

In the multiplicity of bugs, insects, birds,
God with an appetite.

God in the softening of sorrow,
the throwing up of hands in defeat.

God in the pulse, heartbeat,
the drumbeat of the universe.

God in the fragments.

Family Album

1.
My sister loves the photograph
of the first five children of our family,
a beautiful portrait, the youngest standing
in his sailor suit on a pedestal.
She goes on so lovingly that I say,
"It would have been nice if there were
a photograph of all of us." I feel small
saying this, but I want to stand up
for my brother and me. Even now
with my hair graying fast, I'm saying,
"Push over! Make room!" Five children
in a row, a hiatus, then two more.
Mother was 46 and 48. A few snapshots.
Dad driving truck, all those mouths to feed.

2.
My mother told me,
"We hadn't had a baby
for a while; you were
the most wanted baby."
Years later, when I told a counselor,
she said, "You believed her?"

3.
You can tell the sashes of her dress are torn
the way the waist hangs loose on her skinny frame.
There's a ribbon in her hair, tight curls from
the Toni permanent her mother gave her
at the kitchen table one Friday night
while her father watched the boxing matches

and the house rang with the clang of each round ending.
Otherwise that hair would be straight as a plumb line.

There's a big bandage on her left arm from some mishap,
but that smile, the light in her eyes, that girl is glad
to be alive and sitting on the piano bench with her little brother
in short pants, palms on his kneecaps, looking up, enchanted,
the older five behind them, but no one happier than these two,
who knew it could have been otherwise.

Photo

An old negative
never developed
until now: my parents,
ready to walk me
down the aisle
our arms linked.

A poor picture
of my mother,
a good-looking woman,
but here, tired.
My father, handsome,
vibrant as I am.

I cut my mother
out of the photo.
I am pretending
my father and I
were pals. Picture me
with my mother
in a hundred ways,
dancing her around
the kitchen, she,
in her apron. Later on,
in the wheelchair.

There is no photo
of father and daughter
like this, so I made one,
and here we are,
both of us dressed to the nines
a white blaze of orchids
between us.

Rain

Sheets of rain, soak of April,
heavy-falling-down water
running like thieves through the street.

I was born in this month.
When my mother brought me home,
the soles of the children's shoes

were eaten away by the downpour.
Cardboard soles, the rationing
of leather during the war.

Later, my dad took me to Schloff's
for sturdy brown oxfords which would not
disintegrate under any conditions.

Today I smelled the rain-on-dirt smell
fat drops hitting hard scrabble, rain soaking
thick thumb weeds in empty corner lots.

My Dad Comes Back on Grand Avenue

He bought big for the family, cratesful
of peaches from the wholesaler,
meat from the butcher in blood-stained apron.

I followed him up the steps,
watched him bargain, the good-natured
barbs, a way to be with him.

He relished the give and take of it,
the basic transaction of commerce,
I have what you need.

About my street, he'd think, what a waste,
pots of flowers at the door of the boutique,
and who needs an olive oil shop?

He's come back in the easiest
way I knew him, making small deals,
at ease in the world.

What he had to teach me took hold
though I wanted more.

I walk the street, cheerful and suspicious
as he was, wondering what nefarious
deed shut down the restaurant,

leaving the tables set,
napkins fanned like swans
swimming a white sea.

The Only Thing That Happened in 4th Grade

Afterward, I never wanted to be fat again.
Frank and I had to wash the blackboard
before the bell rang at St. Vincent's.

We stood with our backs to the others
at the board, erasing the chalk dust,
then dipping our sponges in the bucket
of water, *working off the weight*, she said.
We tried not to leave stripes, to leave
no trace of the day's lessons,

it was private, eyes only, Frank and me,
and the others watching. Do they remember?
Does Frank? Even writing this,

I see the lie in the plural – *Frank and me,*
we, us. In the cloakroom of shame,
there is always only one small child.

In Memoriam

for Jim White

You died sometime Sunday night
before my letter arrived. It came back marked,
"Return to Sender. Deceased."

My time was Tuesday at 4:00, $15 in cash
to sit at your kitchen table
sipping sassafras tea while you read my poems,
one you marked, *lofty.*

"Write about Frogtown," you told me,
"write about coal yards and railroad tracks,
laundry flapping the clothesline."

What a dowsing that was, a strike deep
into the ground where real poems lived.
Feverish, I wrote you a letter so we could begin.

You were buried like a nobleman.
We sang you out with stout
Episcopalian hymns in the cathedral
and a feast of funeral food
for a lover of sweets.

The great wheel moved forward,
implacable beast,
dumb to your gifts.

Jazz Trumpeter

"You are not who this country says you are."
– Hannabal Lakumbe

His voice is soft
and he stops often.
The young black men
around the table,
fidget with their braids,
sprawl.

Doing the right thing
he says, is harder
than 100 Chinese push-ups.
A pause for push-ups.
The boys take turns
making the triangle
with their hands on the floor,
getting their chins down
into that triangle.

He wears them down
with his voice,
his silence. He waits
for them to find their way
and they do: one
tells of the grandmother
related to Ida B. Wells,
another to Leadbelly.
None of these boys
is nothing.

On their faces,
a sense of calm

as if some confusion
has been ordered,
bodies upright,
hands quiet in their laps.

He takes up the trumpet,
the slow wail,
shows them what to do
with sorrow.

City Trees, Coffee Shop, Spring

Some days trees are all I see,
trunks lined up on the boulevard as I walk,
limbs like the bone structure
of a classic face –
that's the way trees are for me.

Today they're getting fringed in leaves
at the crown. Underneath
there's a huge ball of root that nobody sees
except my son as a five-year old
who drew one exactly as a botanist might,
side view, x-ray vision.

Nobody talks about trees over cappuccino
outside the coffee shop, friends
talking over Friday night's game,
laughing at the score.
A jogger passes me; a car horn shrieks.

Let this Saturday be perfect.
Let nothing terrible happen.
No stray bullets or pedestrian deaths.
Let traffic roll safety toward the freeway.
Let the trees survive, let them be
counted, cared for, oldest residents of the city.

The Catch

Signac painted the fishing boats straight on,
Five of them and a little skiff,
prows forward, masts splicing the air,
flags flying in the breeze of a most
temperate day, clouds, but no rain, the rippling
Atlantic waters contained in the bay.

The people, sticks of black behind the boats,
barely visible, but I bet the whole town
turned out for the send-off, at least one child
fished out, gasping, and the priest, rushing
the planks, wings of his stole flapping
behind him, ready to fling holy water aloft.

But the blessing belongs to the artist
who must have sketched the scene from his own boat
further out, the one he sailed from Mediterranean
port to port, all the way to Istanbul.
He painted a thousand dabs of color
he knew the eye would transform into fish for the catch.

The Blessing of the Tuna Fleet at Croix
Paul Signac
Minneapolis Institute of Arts

Single

Just when I had run
out of anger
when I could have lived
years without a man,
raising kids, filling out
forms, (except the night lilacs
broke open
and loneliness pooled
on the kitchen table)
just when the house was tidy,
you came with your dog, Muffin,
(I had never had a dog)
came with books, notes
in bad handwriting,
thousands of papers,
the spine on the book of life
undone.

Stepdog

I was the only dog she knew
none in the childhood that she remembers.

The best times were riding in the backseat
of the old Plymouth station wagon

spinning down country roads
gravel flying out from the wheels

her face in the fur of my neck
my nose to the wind.

My nose to the wind
her face in the fur of my neck

gravel flying out from the wheels
spinning down country roads

riding in the old Plymouth
the backseat, the best times.

None in the childhood that she remembers
I was the only dog she knew.

To Eugene

I crossed the country, flew straight
over the Atlantic to Madrid,
another plane to Alicante
where a courtly man drove with skill
up and down mountains to the artist house
on Carrer Mare De Deu Del Miracle
where I was welcomed
and shown a room with a single bed
in which I slept through the bells
of Saints Cosmos and Damian
(and the rooster) straight into Sunday
to find the one public phone in the village
along the flank of the church,
and with the noon blaze full upon me,
fished my telephone card
(five euros, 50 minutes) out of my purse,
the salt of sweat blurring my vision,
punched the numbers,
the English number,
the PIN number and your
number which is our
number and got it right.
Hello, you said.
Hello.

The Tour Guide Speaks

I wish you could see children flooding the lobby
jamming up the line, talking, then raising their eyes
to Chihuly's *Sunburst,* "It's on fire!"

They walk the great hall not staying behind me.
giggle at naked Doryphorous,
mimic his stance, spear in hand.

Dogs in a painting distract them. So do
parquet floors that creak; the brass elevator
they love best. "We're in jail!"

Born in the new century, they take it all in –
the figure of Venus four thousand
years old, the portrait of *Frank,* 1969.

Wealth built this museum. You come, I come,
but I wish you could see the children come,
our *spes regis,* hope of the kingdom.

Art Museum

In the deep well
of the rotunda,
a voice fades
and I am alone,
walking among
the bleached heads
of Roman magistrates
and Greek athletes
with parts long-missing.

I've left behind
the small rooms
of my life.
I slip through the great hall,
a pilgrim
like the figures
in this Chinese hanging.
They're climbing a mountain,
lost in the inky lushness
of trees, the steep
winding toward
the summit.

Pilgrim, you who love
the intimate,
what do you seek
in the great temples
of the world
in cathedrals and mosques,
in space large enough
to swallow you?

Numbering the Oaks

1.
I am the sweeper
of acorns on the sidewalk
brown with tannin,
the one gathering up
bones after the storm,
raker of leaves, the burden
of oaks.

Oak trees in front of the house
and behind, one split in two
like the egg division
of twins, branches jutting
into the air,
a savannah of oaks.

2.
My mother-in-law
died on the eve of Halloween.
In the long raking
of leaves, I laid her to rest,
wind sharp around my shoulders.
The comfort of oaks
still standing.

3.
I studied Aristotle in college,
baffled by *treeness, essence of trees.*
I thought I would understand it

by the time I was a senior.
I gave it up for sex
and babies.

Now I understand
in my body –
eyes, tracking the trail
of bark from trunk
to the explosion of limbs;
with my back and hands,
the work of them.

4.

Is it the German in me?
Echo of the forest in the German character
still alive? Lover of trees, of woods.

Every year I grow more attached
until now I am spinning
myth, how they arise
from roots deep in the earth yet fly
into air; how they lose
their innocence in rain
and turn sexual;

but in winter, oh, winter,
without the distraction of leaves
oak trees whisper like giants
to heaven,
one pure
form to another.

Pink Rose in a Slim Green Vase

What told the stem
to stop
and pink to start
curving into hips
heartbreakingly
full?

On the television news,
disaster.
my life:
the world breaking,
rhapsody of the rose.

Crossing the Waters

2017

Hotel

We've brewed the last cup
of coffee. It's time to leave
this room I've come to love
as I love all the rooms
we've slept in, this one
an interior space, purple walls
and white bed, white desk
and shutters that we opened
for the first time this morning
to find the city blurred behind grime.

You sit on the edge of the bed,
steadying yourself. I come sit
by you, side by side, our hands
cupped, looking out the window,
beyond these walls.

There are two truths –
the truth of going forward,
our reveling in the city, and
the truth of loss, of age,
your faltering, our sorrow.

Going Through the Boxes

Getting ready to move,
I'm reading letters I saved,
cards and messages
from children, husbands,
the charm of well-shaped
language, and how they say it,
the handwriting of each,
a fingerprint, my mother's looped
hand for my birthday, signing
for both of them, "Love
from Mother and Dad."

I'm reading the log we kept
when she was bedridden
and he took sick, we spelled
one another and wrote it down,
medication, telephone calls,
a family crisis and comic relief.
Everything recorded, even the bottle
of Scotch brought to the family meeting.

I saved the best, and the best
has weighed me down.
I want to go lighter into the years.
What will I need for ballast against the tide
of old age? Should I save
the anniversary card of the couple
dancing with lamp shades
on their heads? We never danced
like that, but we were joyful.

Leaving the Garden

We should have moved in winter
when there's nothing
for the eye, the garden reduced
to root, tuber, not now
when the life of plants pushes up
and out, the third day
of creation, so good, all good.

We have lived in beauty,
cultivated it, the slender grasses,
the curly crab,
lily-of-the-valley everywhere
flaunting my failure
to arrange them as I wish.

Along the garage, where
snow-on-the-mountain grows wild,
I planted petunias of
deepest scarlet and set small
stones from Superior,
a narrow line of beauty.

Why curse the Jane Austen rose,
that only blossomed the first year
though I fed and pruned it,
checking it each morning.

Hosta, the rhubarb, sexual again,
peonies, and how to leave
the bleeding heart, especially
the white one, tiny bells shifting in wind.

Healer

Seeing you in pain in your chair,
I think of the hour we spent
with the healer in San Cristobal.
For an offering of 40 pesos, he prayed
over you. As he struck you
with a sword of basil,
you pointed to the small of your back
where the devil resides,
wanting relief from the pain.
I bring what I have – pills and water
and a fig for sweetness.

MADONNA

Unlike her son, she does not suffer.
Nothing in her face reveals
her legendary sorrow. She is mother,
goddess, Our Lady of Soledad, Our Lady
of Guadalupe. In the Metropolitan Cathedral,
the very pillars are sheathed in velvet
for her feast day, and in the villages
streamers festoon the trees. But the poor
love her best. No running water
and the cooking shed covered with corrugated
tin but onc whole wall for her statue.
A profusion of candles in deep red glasses,
the rotten and burned-out right next
to the new, as if this multiplicity could stem
a flood of trouble coming down from the mountains,
as if there were protection in the candor
of rotting flowers.

Retrospective: Frida in Merida

"I hope the exit is joyful – and I hope never to return."
– Frida Kahlo

In our hotel, posters of her paintings
line the walls of the lobby. On the way
to the elevator, baby Diego in her arms.

Every painting, a mirror, her life of pain
after the accident. She is queen
of Mexico now, Frida of the unibrow.

Her face makes money –
on Bohemia's *cerveza*, special edition,
her face on a decorative frying pan.

The government has forgiven her affair
with Trotsky and put her face
on the $500 peso bill,

Diego in the dust, far from the catwalk
that connected their houses,
the wheelchair, death mask still in place.

When I stood on the corner in Merida
buses careening, engines revved,
it's her damaged body that haunted me –

stand back, she said to me,
stand back.

Cane

The sidewalks of Merida were narrow and I often walked ahead of Gene, listening for the tap-tap-tap of his cane. One day he asked me to walk behind him and I got mad. To me it seemed an ancient gender practice for the woman to walk behind the man, never ahead, never leading. He said it was wrong of me to not take account of his hardship, that he pushes himself painfully to keep up. I was confused. Should I fight with him or take care of him? After that, I consciously slowed my natural movements and walked behind him. What I saw startled me. How painfully he maneuvered his way forward, how rickety his body had become over the course of our trip. Sometimes I unconsciously forgot and moved ahead before I caught myself and pulled back. I didn't want to see.

A Fragment found in a Drawer

"Merida and the streets are crowded and loud
with trucks and buses and taxis,
leaving room on the sidewalk for only single file,
people edging along light poles and the street.

Years and years ago, South Korea was so crowded,
but the sounds seemed to be of people
and I was young and not handicapped."

Eugene Jax

Overnight Bus

Next to me, you slept,
like the others

snoring softly,
legs sprawled in the aisle,

only the driver
and I awake.

He was making good time,
a long stretch

with no stops,
no human habitation.

I pulled open the curtain –
Stars, a skyful,

of stars, above
and all the way

to the horizon,
the joy of stars

without number,
but fear, too

of the immensity.
We coursed

through the darkness,
I'd never been

where we were going,
never ridden the night bus

getting there.

The Confluence

On the bridge, heading home
from my errands, I see Pike Island,
a verdant arrow of land
where the waters of the Minnesota River
flow into the Mississippi.

The Dakota thought this point sacred,
the center of the earth.

We moved here because of the sickness.
but in the glory of autumn light,
the world is new, water
and land, primeval.

Long or short, this is our time
at the river.

When I walk the river trail,
the ground that they walked,
I remember and ask the ancients
to help us take strength
from the rivers.

Equipment

Deluxe walker, awkward
as a small dinosaur
in our living room,
manual wheelchair, power
wheelchair to come,
paperwork, 18 pages.
A wedge for easier breathing,
gastric tube and its plugs,
gauze bandages, beaker
and syringe, bi-pap machine,
distilled water, the mask
and its proboscis, three
canes, bed rail and
the handicapped sign.

I hide the equipment,
won't let it make any more
inroads than necessary,
even as you lose one
function after another.
When the end comes
these things will remain,
what I cannot love.

I want a private event
after the funeral, just me
and the things in an isolated
spot where, like a witch,
I will burn the combustibles.
Then with the unholy strength
I'm building, I'll hurl the rest
in defiance over a cliff
into the deep.

The Dream of John

Gone, seven years. Last night in sleep
I conjured my brother
back from the dead.

He wore a robe and was
speaking out against war
as he did in his lifetime.

We embraced so naturally,
he in his fullness
before the wasting.

I woke buoyant, so glad,
for my vision, the capacity
to conjure what is gone.

My brother John came back
on his best day, his body easy,
his mind clear.

How much more you, husband,
whom I have known from the blackest of hair
to the white head I saw yesterday

from a distance, you with the walker,
crossing the portico and I thought, who is
that man with the beautiful hair?

You will come back to me.
I will take the shards of memory
and forge you in the furnace

of my awful desire that you live.

Car

The car is totaled from the accident.
We called Al. He's aged since
the last car, but he's buoyant.

Al leaves to finish the paperwork
on the new car, Basque red, which is no
red at all. I wait, looking out the window
where the new car is purring.

It is a beautiful car
and what American is not
happy about a new car?

You've gone home, leaving me
to close the deal. When I was upset
about the accident, you said,
"We can't be concerned about
those things now."

Not so different from our first date,
when you picked me up
in a small station wagon
with a cookie tin on the floor,
driver's side, to keep the rain out.

When Al comes back, I sign
the contract, and it is only
my signature. The aching absence
of your name makes me forlorn.
This the car of my widowhood.

The Wedding

Let me say how much I've loved going out
with you, the two of us, a couple.

I've creased your trousers and ironed the blue shirt
that colors your pale skin. That little section

of wrist below the cuff that drives me crazy in a man
drives me crazy now. I've misted the air

with perfume and walked through it
the way French women do.

I have on "eyes" as my mother would say, and
sterling silver at my wrist.

You're tired and your arms hurt, supporting yourself
on the walker, but I know you will relish

greeting people, a social man, you'll laugh, full-throated
again. People will say to one another,

"He still looks good," and you do. This wedding,
the granddaughter of old friends, may be our last.

Soon I'll stop trying so hard to keep the old life.
We'll both give in to the disease, just not yet.

We look as good as we're ever going to look,
and the sun is unexpectedly warm for March.

Out we go.

When Leaf Buds Open on the Trees

A soft green appears and if it rains then,
hard, the young leaves drink it in without
hesitation, and even the bark of the most
ordinary tree is erotic, dark after rain.

The branches stand out, outlined in black
like my childhood drawings, an early
fascination with structure, with contrast,
the bark against the shine of leaves.

Even when the trees bush out, fulsome
with leaves, it stays with me,
the intricate fretwork, the road clear
right up to the top, the tree revealing itself.

Saint Francis in the Desert

Drawn into the strange light
that turned the rocky cliff jade green,

Francis left the grotto, his sandals,
the skull perched above the book of Holy Writ.

In the field nearby, a young donkey sees it, too.
Everything faces immanent light except the hare,

so plump, content to remain close to the friar's
wooly cloak. All the elements of life, clouds,

Sister Water from the spout, Brother Heron nearby
are present as Francis stands transfixed,

arms wide, his torso, his whole body
a triptych of reverence, of transformation.

If you look closely, you can see the stigmata
on his hands and that's the heavenly Jerusalem

in the background, but the force of the painting
is Francis in radiance. This is more than technique.

Bellini knew this state or he could not have painted
Francis full-strength in the sway of it,

so that whatever the viewer brings to the painting,
coming upon it, as I did and stopped to tears,

we want, like Brother Hare, to stand with Francis.

Saint Francis in the Desert
The Frick Museum
New York City

Sunday Morning in the Old City

For the peace of Jerusalem pray: may peace reign in your walls, in your palaces, peace! – *Psalm 121*

I.

Through olive groves and the amphitheatre where rock bands
blasted the night, we climbed to Jaffa gate into the Old City,

the grated shops with their gunnysacks plump with almonds
and lentils, casks of jewelry, tunics and rugs hanging like
laundry, waiting

for the hot breath of the bargaining to come. Quiet as thieves
and as quick, we passed under a canopy of lush bougainvillea,
and heard the cry

of a baby, the clink of silverware, the interior life above the
shops; past the Church of the Holy Sepulchre, the cavernous
vault

eerie with the glow of red votives, wax from a thousand
candles, past the narrow checkpoint where Israeli soldiers
inspected our bags before

we entered the plaza of the Wailing Wall, where we stood
with the Jews yesterday, touching our foreheads to the stone,

up to the summit where the golden Dome of the Rock
shines over all Jerusalem.

II.

Jerusalem, Jerusalem
the very name embedded as fossil in my mind,
ancient stone, city of the psalms,

"Jerusalem, My Happy Home,"
the hymn we sang at my mother's funeral,

Jerusalem, where all the streets
are a Via Dolorosa,

Jerusalem, crossroads of traffic with the divine,
mystical city

where Abraham lay wood to make human sacrifice
of his only child,

where Mohammed mounted
the ladder to heaven,

where the Jews gather
at their holiest site to pray at the one wall
remaining of Temple Mount.

I walked the esplanade, looking out over the city,
the blindingly white stone,
of modern Jerusalem on one side,
on the other, the Garden of Gethsemane
where Jesus prayed for courage
and the bleached gravestones
of two millennia shine in the morning sun.

I stood on the ramparts
like the ancients looking out over
the whole known world.

Family

Awake, in the middle of the night
I think of my brother's family
not seen since his funeral
and my sister's family not seen
since she died. The loss comes to me
as a great shearing, cutting
a wide swath, layer after layer
of family gone, the terrible
winnowing out, the thinning.

I want them all back,
as we were, lively, troubled,
generous or not, I want us
to laugh and sing again,
this oversized family with no
house big enough to hold us
so we gathered in summer
at the picnic or at weddings
and now at funerals of which
even one is too many.

Summer

When the rains come,
oak bark blackens to a bold
calligraphy, small tufts
of leaves fall, an afterthought.

The peonies we picked
before the downpour
bend in fullness before
the letting go begins.

Oak and peony,
and what of our arms
which narrow
to the tender bones of wrist
before widening to hands
that hold and let go,
hold and then let go.

Evensong

Walking the river trail,
I see one boat, one fisherman
on the river, his back
against low sun.
I think of the Dakota,
the early ones in their river
solitude, knowing the currents
and when to head to shore.
Darkness narrows the river's
silver path. I'm heading
home myself, up the steep hill,
a little breathless. A chill
from the woods touches my arm.
How we come to evening.

Now I Live Among Old Trees

2020

The Suitcase

I've seen how they age and sicken,
move to be near children or not,
alone, widowed or just alone.

They carry the suitcase of loss,
and now I am with them,
and you are one of the ghosts

of dislocation, your name freighted
with the weight of memory,
you and the others who've died,

floating above our lives
neither past nor present,
the eternal now.

Appetite

Small bowls of food now, what use
the yellow bowl from Italy, all the ceremonial
dishes in the cabinet.

No meal I would have recognized.
Always serve three things,
I told the children, and one of them green.

Now half a banana, cream to fatten you,
soft food you won't choke on,
the man who loved tempura.

You cooked so many of our meals
and now you can't stand at the counter
and are hopeless to find the good knife.

This most human ritual of food,
shopping, preparing it, eating, and what
to do with the leftovers, reduced

to small bowls of pudding and the daily
feeding of guaranteed nutrients
through a tube. "Delicious," you tell me.

When Spring Came

A cancer. Mine. A cauldron
of trouble, a pox on both of us.
Will I live?

I am a mountain being mined
deep in the interior.
My daughter holds my hands.

Night terrors, but by day,
protocols in orderly sequence,
stage, port, chemo cocktail.

My children deliver me
into the care of kindly nurses
and stay with me,

close companions in the smallest
of rooms. I was someone I didn't
recognize but they did.

Talking to Sparrows

The first days, from bed to sofa,
everywhere pillows to catch me,

and in-between watching my hair,
barely combing it, waiting

for the fallout which comes
on day 13, just as the nurse said,

hair with no anchor, the chemo
killing follicles as it kills

cancer cells, hair on the sofa,
on pillows, chairs, I open the balcony,

fling it by fistfuls out on the grass,
shake my scarves, my sweater, take it,

I say to the sparrows, take it all,
make something of this.

Fast Food

We're eating caramel sundaes at McDonald's
as a car pulls up, a woman hurries in
after her boys, already jumping
from one booth to another.

Two guys talk nearby, one of them
gesturing, making a point that we can't hear
because the ice machine
is making a frappe'.

Another woman arrives, so alive
in her blue sleeveless shirt, checking
the menu overhead, talking
on her phone, getting the order straight.

The clerk with the least seniority sweeps
the place. We're all just living a summer eve.
The sun is going down on us, leaving
the softest darkness in the trees.

HORTICULTURE

The red chair in the corner
where he spends his days
among books,

ice water, a salt shaker
in case she cuts up an apple,
a bell to call her, but the prize

is the African violet. He used to garden
Asian lilies, peonies, tomatoes,
bleeding heart, but one

African violet stands in for them all,
the indigo flowers, the feathery
leaves, a lively presence among

the inanimate. He tends it,
manicure scissors to cut the dead blossoms,
a little gardening every morning.

Summer's Mending

Time of gin and tonic, of opening
and closing of windows,
the drone of the air conditioner.

Time of gardening, seeding the grass,
pulling weeds, keeping the impatiens,
petunias, the lilies watered.

Time of the thunder of acorns,
the sidewalk dark with tannin,
the walks I take, every day a little farther.

Time of healing,
of sun and heat and light,
thick with green.

Triptych: Cemetery

1.
Driving home from a late meeting,
I pass the cemetery where your ashes
will be buried.

I pass the gate, drive the fence line,
slowing the car down.

There are no streetlights in the land
of the dead.

How can I leave you there?

2.
Your new neighborhood has rules. I read today that if
I get an upright stone, I can plant flowers. Your spot
is too fresh for a stone, the ground still soft. Winter is coming,
despite the brilliance of oak and maple. I walk nearby
to see the grave of my former student, Will, who went down
with Wellstone's plane. His family left a pumpkin for him.
You'll have one next year. At the top of the hill, a valiant angel
lifts her hand in blessing and all around are the mausoleums
of the wealthy and the settlements of Hmong graves.
Your neighborhood has an enviable diversity, unmatched
anywhere else in the city.

3.
The path to your grave is snow-packed
from my boots and studded
with oak leaves, bronze against white
like fallen stars.

The path I'm making from the car
to your grave is a straight line,

nothing like the circular tracks of rabbit,
fox, one who leaps, a cloven foot.

They live here too. I am the outsider,
making my own way, a desire line,

what architects call the paths
we humans take, making it clear

where we want to go, and where I
want to go is to you. I dust off your wreath

of snow and tell you bad news
which you cannot help me with.

I have good news, too. The wild turkeys
are back, pecking at the corn I throw out,

comic heads above their sculpted bodies,
feathered precisely, a deeper bronze

than the oak leaves. We always
welcomed them, called them to our balcony

our animal comfort.

The Eugene Letters

1.
My Dear Eugene

Alone at table, the humblest of meals,
soup and bread, a mat under my bowl,
knife and spoon on the right, the way
my mother showed me.

She learned at the restaurant where she worked
and maybe got pointers from her sister,
our Auntie Anne, who cooked for Louie Hill
up on Summit Avenue.

I keep the pattern. I sit down, a coffee-stained
New Yorker on my left where you sat,
and I think if you ever appear, beloved shade,
you will come when I am at table.

2.
My Dear Eugene

I like to sit alone in a church,
not an intimate space, nothing convivial,
but old, magisterial, a terrible crucifix,
cold comfort.

I'm starting over, trying to build
a life for myself
instead of the life we had.

I've moved to a new home
with no memory of you
the hall and doorway too narrow
for the wheelchair.

In the years of your sickness,
I didn't see myself aging until
you were gone. Tell me, love,

do you know and would you say,
if there is time to make a new life?
Or should I just stay home with your
photo in every room?

3.
My Dear Eugene

Not a photo of the two of us
but this one of you in Istanbul,
standing, hands in pockets,
your travel bag across your chest,
the Sea of Mamara behind you,
eyes bright, you, standing between
two continents.

Maybe heaven for you is Istanbul, the city
you loved, and just as you went to Istanbul
without me, you've gone on again.
And just as we went together later on,

maybe Istanbul is where I'll join you
and we'll see again the dervishes whirling,
white robes flying, steadied it seemed
by the tall tan hats they wear
like a cap on a bottle of fizz.

Or this is all romance and what I have
is this photo of you far away. I keep you here
in my bedroom by the desk
where I write this poem.

Like the Japanese guardian figures
outside the temple, you keep watch,
don't you, love? You hear me ask each day
for what I need to go on without you.

4.
My Dear Eugene

Younger, when I lost
my way as a writer,
distracted by what
I didn't win,
I pulled myself back
to the making
of a poem,
how intimate
the mind's interior,
my hand
writing the words,
the moment
of getting it right.

I do that now
when I think of
losing you again, not
your body, already
gone, but you
in my mind where you
have always
flourished.

I pull you close,
return to the state
of our near faces,
your eyes the color
of November waters,
the deep knowledge
the body imprints
on the mind
and I rest there.

Prosper

Gasquet on Cezanne: "He had no real friends except trees."

1.
A cottonwood anchors me,
its crown fills the windows.
It has all the room it needs, a generosity
of limbs above the double trunk
and roots that break the ground and run
like streams from its circumference.
Sometimes when I awake, the tree is bronze,
until the angle of sun shifts,
then the leaves glint and sway like tinsel,
a giant of a tree I have named *Prosper*.

2.
When the day's work is done, when I'm reading
in the quiet or watching a mystery,
I can't keep my eyes from twilight in the west,
the darkness in the tree long before the sky
eases into night, bands of amber and rose,
a slow fading.

It settles me in my new life. Prosper's crown, thick
with darkness, arches over a house in its shadow,
small, lamplight within, ghostly white against the dark.

3.
I showed my friend my view of the tree –
she said, "That is your mountain."

Like a mountain or a body of water,
it is a place for the eye to rest

and where the eye rests, I see again
my younger self, my mother, a husband,

a shirt stolen from the clothesline two houses ago.
Then other winds bring me back, summer storm shakes

my wild unsettled friend.

Now I Live Among Old Trees

The college could have been
another country, unfamiliar streets,
so many beautiful trees, old
trees, trees allowed to widen into sky
bluer in that part of town.

I took the bus until I met the others
who didn't fit in, alone as I was,
watching the ranks of girls
hug each other, at ease among
such trees.

Not fitting in, that was our bond,
stuck together, smoking cigarettes,
studying for tests in the smoker,
not the library, each book, like the trees,
settled and quiet.

I went to a fine school for women
and graduated, thinking privilege
belonged to others. Like an arrow,
my life took off – the friends
who helped me in the crossing,

I never saw them again.
I never did.

July 4th

The cemetery gate was locked,
when I went to visit you today
in memory of all those crazy 4ths,
when you fried up four chickens
the morning of the picnic, grease
spitting, flour spilling, an occasional
sonofabitch and then we gathered
under the yellow canopy and
when Mary Lou, the oldest, came
we could eat, but not before
she gathered us in a circle, wider
every year, to sing *My Country,*
'Tis Of Thee. Later on, the music
started, Larry on guitar (still with us),
and Janet, (gone now) singing,
while you dozed in the lawn chair,
tired from the chickens, but
awake for the egg toss at the end
of the picnic. We packed up,
car doors slamming and straggled
home, bug-gy and fat, to the slippery
floor, glad for the quiet, going
to bed, the back and forth of the day
jokes, slights, and falling asleep
to fireworks in the distance and
the illegal ones next door: Boom.

Heating Season

for Mary Lou Karp

Early October and the furnace kicks in,
earlier than it did when you lived
on Cook Street, alone, retired,
sweaters keeping you warm,
buying diabetes strips with money
that should have bought groceries.
All your economies come back to me
in the autumn chill.
Your life made me sad sometimes,
you, a single mom, seven kids,
until I was a single mom and then
I learned from you. Here's the revelation:
Sister, I think you lived the way
you wanted to, husbanding your resources.
You lay aside enough money to pay
your nursing home bills, and when
you died there was money for your children.
Sometimes I picked you up from work
and dropped you off at the bank,
and you never said a word
about salting away money, not a burden,
but pride in taking care of yourself
with enough left for the word that conjures
spacious lawns and porticoes:
by damn, you left an ESTATE.

Talking Books

for Tim O'Brien

I ask them what they're reading
in English class. My grandchildren
and I talk books in the car.
One is doing a map of the island
in *Lord of the Flies,* another
an essay on *Gatsby.*
English teachers hard at it,
as I was, suffering a pile
of papers over spring break,
pulling young minds
into the drama on the page.

Copulating dogs in Steinbeck,
Norah slamming the door in Ibsen,
Odysseus outrageously unfaithful,
we read it all in class and talked and I'm
still at it in the car, talking books,
looking at the road ahead.

After I drop them off, I remember
Will, last seat, 3rd row,
who loved baseball, the best
pitcher the school had in years.
His turn to read aloud,
we're on the last chapter
of *The Things They Carried.*
He surprised himself, never
looking up to see whose turn
it was next, the rhythm of prose
so unbroken and grace-filled,
he read right to the end.

When he lifted his head,
his eyes were soft, he knew
he had done something extraordinary.
We were quiet, all of us quiet,
then burst into applause.

Plainsong

for Kate

My first days of chemo she brought
vivid blossoms from her garden,
the opposite of sick.

My only work those long days
to bring fresh water and cut the stems.
Being natural as rain, they did not last

but their frail beauty anchored me.
In the austerity of nausea, a bouquet of lilies,
and bush roses, not so red as cherry.

On the day radiation started,
when I put on the mask that bolted me
to the table, hydrangea. Three varieties.

My poem for Kate is plain – I know only
common names. She knows their specific names,
the sound of them like Baroque fancies.

In my time of cancer, that long summer,
I remember the treatment, yes,
and yes, armfuls of lilies with dark centers.

Philando Castile

In that cathedral atop the highest hill in Saint Paul,
we gathered for Philando. He came on a white catafalque
drawn by horses, his coffin carried up the hill by pallbearers
in white suits into the nave of the Cathedral, filling
with mourners, his family, his neighbors, his co-workers
from school, senators, mayors, thousands of people
came to his funeral, they filled that church which that day
was everybody's church. Beautiful black men
ushering up and down the aisles, beautiful black women
in white hats, some of them plumed, and all of us, ordinary
people who wanted to say, "No. Not this man." If ever
change could happen, we felt it might with this death,
this ignominious death that destroyed the scales of justice.
There at the center of the city, in the eye of the crisis,
we were together, white and black to hear the gospel choir rock
the Cathedral, to sing full-throated, three thousand voices
filling that holy space, holy because we came together
for Philando who should have lived a long life, should
have been there to bury his mother and instead she buried him
like a nobleman, not in the Baptist church, but at the Cathedral
on the highest hill in the city, and like a lord, he was carried out
down one hundred steps and we all formed an honor guard to watch
his coffin descend and be placed upon the catafalque
to ride down Selby Avenue, his mourners following on foot,
to his school where the funeral food was barbeque and lasted
all that July afternoon.

In Life I Was of Modest Size, in Death I am the Garden

I had nerves all my life, only one
pup, she was pretty,
but I liked the couple better.

No sitting on top of the sofa,
but I did when they left.
Every car that passed,
I looked, hoping.

I had a red leather leash.
She walked me on
Grand Avenue where people stopped
to admire my spots.

She wasn't patient. Even if
I was afraid of other dogs, we were kin.
I wanted to smell –
she wanted exercise.

He took me to the country
where I could chase wild turkeys,
but I heard him say I was racist
because I barked at black people.

I meant no harm and would have
let them pet me
if I saw them more often.

The last years she put a sheet
over the sofa and I watched for them

on 100% cotton.
I died at home.
A woman came and held me
with such tenderness
that I never saw the needle.

They buried me in the backyard
where fern and hosta thrive.

World Enough and Time

New Poems

"And love's the
sacred name
for loneliness"
– Christian Wiman

"My spiritual life is so much a part of
my intellectual life and my feeling life
that it is really impossible to keep it
out of my work."
– Jane Kenyon

Matins

Everything Rises and Falls

The branches of the trees move up
and down, like the movement
of small animals.

Waking in the morning, the tree
of my body, the small
animal of my breath.

High Up: Sunrise

An old moon thinning in the west above trees,
copper for a moment,
bright and brief.

Eastward, the cathedral emerges from darkness,
behind an urban forest
and farther back, the cemetery.

The buildings downtown break the tree line,
piled like turrets of a kingdom,
and that long absence in the landscape
is the Mississippi River.

Nearer, streetlamps fade like moonlight,
a garbage truck lumbers in,
an engine starts, neighbors heading to work
and already the Amazon van is circling.

Looking up, the sky curves
at the horizon, holding us every
ordinary day.

The Garden

A renter now, I miss it,
the bang of the back door,
checking for green shoots
each morning. Then I remember,
I own a parcel of land
at the cemetery. I have
monument privileges.
Your stone is modest, but
above ground. I can plant.
I dig and sweat and pull up
clumps of grass, laying
the groundwork. Others
have geraniums, but for you,
darling, a line of scarlet
and white petunias
just as I planted on Goodrich
between the garage
and the sidewalk,
a narrow line of beauty.

Pandemic Check List

The coffins of Italy
Refrigerated trucks for the dead in NYC
Churches, theatres, stores, locked down
Suspicion
Rants
Dr. Fauci gets a security detail
Pink slips, go home
Students, go home
Women leave their jobs, go home
Zoom, getting it right, clicking the right buttons
Takeout, plastic, Styrofoam
Sweat pants
Masks, disinfectant,
Appointments online, more zoom
Netflix, binge TV
Brief grocery store runs
Empty shelves, hoarding
Six feet stickers on the floor, ropes
Plexiglas shields
No lipstick, no haircuts
The sudden appearance of barrettes
Liquor stores an essential service
Holiday dinner alone
Loneliness, finding a pod
The sick, the old, isolated
Families waving from a window
No hugs, no embrace, masks and shield
Death notices, no funerals
No singing, no blowing of instruments
Pee at home
Keep your breath to yourself.

Easter Dinner

Lamb with rosemary and garlic,
a lemon confection for desert.

I look out at the fierceness of snow
blocking my view of the tree,

everything odd, snowstorm
in April, a holiday dinner for one,

a muted solidarity, so many alone,
the circle broken.

Breaking out: Minnehaha Falls

I walk the path, leaving
my tedious solitude.
Not disease, not virus
with its stealth,
but the rush of water,
untamed, crashing
from the precipice, down,
down, a wild pitch
filling the creek.
the surge of it, knocking
the barricade, its power
uncontained, but further
down, the water settles,
flows with more decorum
to the mouth of the Mississippi
where other waters gather,
flowing south, all waters, to the sea.

April Birthday

Sprightly pansies, deep purple,
a succulent garden,
a birthday cake made of flowers.

Fig, fern, and big green flourish,
how they love
the lengthening light.

I've seen the masked family
from a distance, and you, husband,
even farther away.

Here on the sixth floor,
I am at the center
of a hidden garden.

The year is at the spring.
I'm going to live among flowers,
in a fragrant enclosure.

The First Live Performance of the Saint Paul Chamber Orchestra

Lake Como, an open pavilion,
Corinthian pillars hold up the roof,
a breeze and birds dipping in
and out over the lake like children
playing tag.

We sit, benches, folding chairs,
all our flaws on display,
the heat, the heat, no one
dresses up or even covers up,
a sea of shorts on skinny legs,
varicosities, the body as pudding,
we're jockeying beer and wine,
a basket of fries or tacos.

The musicians gather and long
before they're ready, we're clapping
and whistling, starved for live music.

A nod from the master, the hush
as the program begins,
Vivaldi, then Handel, Viet Cuong,
Walker, Beethoven, short pieces,
a generosity of solos.

Afterward, instruments packed away,
a word, a wave, we find our cars,
board the buses, leave the pavilion open
for the swoop and sail of birds
riding the echo.

For the Poets

I am living. I remember you. – Marie Howe

There are no obsequies.
You may not even know
of the death if you skip
obituaries.

Carol Connolly
Mike Finley
Tom Heie
Scott King
Elissa Cottle
Kevin Fitzpatrick
Ethna McKiernan
Mimi Jennings
Barbara Sperber

They wrote, withstood rejection,
wrote anyway, published
or didn't, enlarged
our tribe with their antics,
wit, sorrow, high spirits
and sheer inventiveness.

They passed quietly, cloistered,
our tribe of bards.
They mattered.

Relic

A sliver of wood
encased in a locket.
a fragment of the true cross.

My father pinned it on the gown
near my mother's heart
whenever she seemed near death.

Hers a long dying, his, a matter
of hours. After they both died,
I asked for the relic.

My brother said that if you gathered
all the relics of the true cross together,
it would rival Noah's ark.

The only truth I know is my mother's heart
and how we used everything
in our power to keep her with us.

Jesus, hearing of the death of John the Baptist

When Jesus received the news from the apostles,
he withdrew by boat to a lonely place. – Matthew 14: 13

My mother did that when Larry went to Vietnam.
She went to the basement, a cave of sorrow.

Partings, terrible and permanent, we turn
inward, let the laundry, the trash accumulate.

Jesus relented when he saw the crowds
that followed him, sick and hungry.

He fed them from a few baskets of bread
and two fish – that was the divine part.

My mother lit candles for the dying and the sick,
my brothers and sisters do that too.

I forget to light candles, but I never
forget the leave-taking.

Perspective, January

I saw Pissarro's *Place du Theatre Francais*
which he painted high up
from his hotel window.

Every detail of the coaches
in the square below,
black and glistening with rain.

Farther back, the smudging of windows
and horses, even farther,
the faint lines of the Opera House
which up close dazzles.

I was afraid.
Are you the Opera House, am I
the painter?

Your life, our life receding,
growing fainter, losing detail and now
the calendar turns, another year
since we were in that hotel together.

Place du Theatre Francais, Paris, Rain, 1898
Camille Pissarro
Minneapolis Institute of Arts

Shadow

The garage door opens
like a stage curtain.
I drive out and
there it is
the shadow of my car,
a bi-location,
my double?
If it stayed longer,
I could befriend it
but these glimpses,
the light just so,
weighing nothing,
but weighty,
the same scene
but with
all the detail
erased,
a car, someone
at the wheel.
Emptied of me.

Composition in Black and White

The huge crown of the cottonwood,
branches bare against the sky.
The hill behind heaped with snow
clean of boot prints.

The groundskeeper's house
sheltered by the great tree in summer,
small and alone now.

Other houses angle sideways
peaked roofs white
with snow. Bare tree
and evergreens, as if each yard
got an allotment.

From my window, a hamlet,
houses and trees, a road
out to the world.

The Noonday World

Lynching Memorial, Duluth, 1920

An event has happened upon which it is difficult to speak and impossible to remain silent. – Edmund Burke

Not a tourist area. A public square
in the heart of the city,
where the jail stood,
a garden, hallowed words.
The three figures, dressed now,
sculptured in black relief.

Elias Clayton, circus worker
Elmer Jackson, circus worker
Isaac McGee, circus worker

Did they think, how lucky –
easy work, regular meals,
and so many brothers?

The young woman said she was raped.
Alarmed, just a few gathered
in the afternoon, outside the jail
but the crowd grew.
A man drove his truck
through town, "necktie party,
downtown!"

Elmer, Elias, and Isaac could hear
the mob grow by the hour in their cell.
10,000 by night fall.

The electricity went out, the jail
breached, walls gave way.
Elias, Elmer, and Isaac hid in the corner

under a blanket. They were hanged
from the light post to the roar
of the mob's approval.

She recanted, but they were already
dead, dumped in unmarked graves
in Park Hill Cemetery
in the poor people's section.

The story went underground,
a foul silence except for Negro parents
who told their children,
"Don't think everything is fine. The veneer
is awful thin." Many left the city.
Hard to find a home if you stayed.

Seventy-one years, their remains
unmarked. Generations came and went
until one man, a few and then many
rose up to remember, to mark
the space with a garden
and words of fury and wisdom.

Buried them again under a walnut tree
together but separate,
in the poor section, which they were:

Elias Clayton
Elmer Jackson
Isaac McGee

With thanks to Michael Fedo,
The Lynchings in Duluth

Hunger

Yesterday, the refrigerator held
bottles of hot sauce and milk. Sour.
I used up everything in the freezer,
frugal me.

By evening the refrigerator light shone
on my wealth – plump oranges, fresh
cream, frozen pizza, pasta salad
from the deli. Empty, then full.

Did my mother feel this satisfaction
when she finished canning peaches
and tomatoes, lining the jars up
in the fruit cellar to sustain us for winter?

No steam of August for me,
I fill the gas tank of the refrigerator
at the store, cook sometimes,
and eat ice cream every night.

In the morning, I read the newspaper
and see a woman from Ethiopia (Yemen? Syria?)
holding a baby whose skin barely covers bones.
Almost every morning, another child.

The photos stay with me. I think
of the photographers recording this,
day after day. When they get home
they go grocery shopping.

I send money and prayers,

but I don't know what to do
about the having, the not
having, the great sorrow of our age,

what to do about the *knowing*.

Repairs

The remote can be fixed, the eyeglasses
repaired, insignificant, but satisfying,
a sense of the day moving forward.

But how to fix the world, the miserable
refugee camps, the tent cities of my town,
polluted water, no blue sky.

The sense
of things gone wrong.

Peace House

The only building left standing on the block next to the freeway. Inside, folding chairs line the room, people already sitting, moving around, getting coffee. On the walls are the rules, what will get you thrown out and for how long. Everything is simple here and unadorned except for a few tired Christmas decorations, but there's light and heat and soon there will be food.

The discussion is about to begin. Thomas locks the door so there are no interruptions, unless someone bangs on it, angry at missing the deadline. But for now, it's peaceful, no one's drunk or high, one man sleeps, but he's not snoring and the rest seem alert. They all have hats and gloves, gifts of a church organization.

Now the leader asks for news and Sharon says how three people who were lighting their cigarettes in the street at dawn were hit by a truck. Her husband is one of them and she's looking for a ride to the hospital. The leader says he'll give her a lift. Then the topic for discussion, the giving of gifts, the complications of giving and receiving. So many of those gathered have broken and missing teeth, rheumy eyes and bodies older than their years, but they talk about the uneasy transaction of receiving gifts. Suddenly, Stanley starts speaking, his voice ringing out, his mind ablaze. He says that he always knows when the spirit is wrong behind a gift, but he doesn't let that stop him. "I let the Lord turn it around. The Lord turns it around!"

The leader directs the traffic of their voices and they all get heard. It's his birthday, and so they all sing the birthday song that everyone knows. Then Al brings platters of fried chicken, bowls of potatoes and salad, trays of Christmas cookies and sets them on low tables in the middle of the room. After lunch, the door is unlocked and the stragglers come in out of the cold.

Key: A Found Poem

After he was given a bed
in a hotel room, his mind cleared.
He's rested and mad at himself

for the choices he's made.
He said we have no idea how exhausting
life is without a home, finding a bed

at the shelter and if they're full,
riding the light-rail all night
or stumbling in the cold until dawn.

Not a partition, not a plastic sheet
hanging between cots: A key.
A bathroom. A bed with clean linen.

He locks the door. Eleven hours straight
the first night, fourteen the second.
He sleeps.

Arbeit Macht Frei

The old survivors
are walking under
the gate at Auschwitz.

A dip in each step,
the stalls where they slept,
gold from their teeth.
Auschwitz, a museum.

The carry the memory
of the camp In their bodies,
the ink on their arms still
legible.

They've come to honor
the lost, before they die
their natural deaths.

The old survivors
are walking under
the gate at Auschwitz.

Midway Airport

Hours to go before I board the plane.
I'm in-between, untroubled,
holding my coat which smells
of wet wool from walking Michigan
in the rain. A smell of bus stations,
a bachelor uncle down on his luck.

Coffee and a sweet in the commons,
among those who never look up
from machines and a group of Black guys
around a table, jovial, sure of their welcome.

I stop to see the Battle of Midway exhibit,
a dive bomber suspended
from the ceiling. I didn't know it was the battle
that turned the tide of World War II.

I didn't know there was a yoga room either
and a chapel. In the yoga room, a couple
cross over to me, apologizing, saying
they are finished praying.

I expected the bars, the pizza, but not
praying, not a dive bomber, the airport a little
microcosm in the heart of the country,
Chicago, the great crossroad of the nation.

A young boy plops down on my coat.
I say, that's my coat. His sister comes
and he moves over crowding me.
I wonder if I should move, but there's
the boarding call.

I stand and the boy points
to the floor where my locket has fallen.
I thank him and smile, no longer
the crabby lady who crowded them.

The rain turns to slush on the runway.
My breath catches as we fly through fog,
but rising, a star of pure light appears
through a filament of rose.

The Coat

I hung the black wool coat
on a wooden hanger, wrapped
a soft scarf around the neck,
put a leather glove in each pocket.

I hung it in the closet to give
to our friend who never had
such a coat and asked for it.

The coat reminds me of the dignity
with which you carried yourself
even when you were loose and funny.

My elderly neighbor, a widow
who lived next door two houses ago,
kept such a coat in her closet
to warn off intruders.

A widow myself, I thought,
"Should I keep it?"
But who wants a mannequin
when you've had the man?

Poem for Singles

My sister, divorced, told me,
years ago, that marriage is a novel
and being single, short stories.
I see her point. Sometimes
being single is a poem, often
a limerick.

I miss the depth of me and thee, love,
(that's gone). The world is coming to me
in a new way.

My garage mate sees my book
on the front seat. I've never met anyone
who read *My Bright Abyss.*
The stranger who saved me when I forgot
the front door would be locked,
a bad end to a beautiful night.

I'm writing an anthology of tales
and counting the blessing of it,
what John Brantner (God rest)
called the caravan or Chaucer,
stories told on pilgrimage.

Graduate

for Elijah

A shining young man, the one who rode
the wheelchair through the halls
ratcheting it up and sideways,
who clicked every button, moved every dial,
who sat heavily on my lap as a baby.

Like Whitman, you contain multitudes.
Those lanky limbs hide your former lives,
the time zooming too fast and I can't
share this with your grandfather who tracked
your growth with such affection. He dies
and I age as you go forward like your brother,
your cousins, your mates, all of you eager
to turn the dial on the world.

The Composition of Evening

Park Point, Duluth

1.
The blast of the ore boat,
one long, two short and as the engineer
calls back, the counterweights move down
and the Lift Bridge goes up, a feat
of exquisite balance.

Masabi Miner glides into harbor
riding low, all 1000 feet, longer than my city block.
The cars on either side of the traffic gates
wait for the lion of commerce to pass.

2.
I am a tourist and not. This is
my daughter's city, her job
to be tough and tender,
the city struggling, hardscrabble
neighborhoods and the prosperous
four-square houses which stand
against the wind.

How she loves its streets, hills
rising up from Lake Superior
like loaves of bread,
a mythical landscape.

3.
I cross the road each morning
to walk the beach and greet
the dogs, walking smartly.
If I'm alone, I sing, "My Lord,
what a morning!"

4.
One morning at the beach I saw
a woman on crutches enter the water,
a guide at her side.
Then she gave over the crutches
and dove in.

5.
In my little house, I live alone
and not alone. My children come and go
as they did in childhood.
Leggy grandsons bound the steps
to the deck dangling car keys
and bringing me pizza.

The man upstairs rises before dawn
to water the planters downtown –
baskets of blossoms, colorful
as hats at a royal wedding.
He does the work of the flowers.

6.
Friends stay overnight and we see
each other's nighties. One stares off,
embracing the lake while the film
of her life unrolls. Another speaks,
two speak, the silence when they're gone.
I walk to the queue and watch
the waves push against the seawall,
and explode into air like our laughter.

7.
Toward evening at the beach
parents pack up, shake out blankets,

but their children – the toddler spooning the lake
into a hole in the sand, won't look up.

8.

On the deck I watch twilight settle in the trunks
of the trees, but the crown of the pine
still holds the light. The neighbor's dog is quiet,
part of the composition of evening.
Faint birdsong, not morning's call.

9.

City dweller, I love the horizontal line,
the sky, the lake, a seamless line of water,
not the wild horses of yesterday.
The beach is empty except for a figure
crouched in prayer at the edge of the water.

Yoke

A trip to a pillared city in a rented house
with my adult children.

In my bedroom downstairs, I hear them crossing
between rooms, stomping, laughing.

During the day, we tour Lincoln at rest, Jefferson
standing, city of museums, what we got right

and the documentation of what was wrong
from the beginning, and still wrong.

Pansies in bloom yesterday, snow falling today
at home. We're back, they're running things,

classrooms, cities. I don't run things anymore,
but I still gather. Five days together,

long after the hard years. Odd custody arrangements,
divorce, remarriage, mine,

their marriages and the grandchildren asking,
"Why do we have so many grandparents?"

I'm soaking my feet. Peaceful.
The yoke of family held.

What I have

for Janet

When I play the piano now, I remember
sitting next to you, the way you pressed
the keys, chords stately and full and when
I get the notes right, I touch the keys that way.

I eat my supper on the chair where you sat
recording the numbers for the doctor
in a small notebook. It's from that chair
that I call in my prescriptions and pay bills.

I have the recording of our dad singing hymns
at the cathedral. You paid for an hour
with the organist so that he could shine.
Certain hymns, spirituals.

Still, what I want is to sit with you again
on the back porch. The nurse left us alone
for a few minutes. We sat side
by side, looking into the garden,
saying nothing.

Ash Wednesday

Remember, Christian, you are dust and unto dust
you shall return.

No ashes today, the city is closed down
for the Pandemic, the only thing open
is the natural world where I walk in the cold,
with my friend whom I do not hug.

I think how lucky that my husband,
who died before the virus hit,
did not die alone.

He liked Ash Wednesday, the bracing
reminder of death. The last years
we gave each other ashes.
I burnt paper, reduced it to ash.
He smudged my forehead and I
smudged his.

This year, I forgot that he was already ash
and thought to bring ashes to the cemetery.
That's how alive he is to me.

Motel: Note to Self

Do not stay again in a room so large.
Two queen beds, when you need a single,
all those pillows meant to comfort lovers
who use the other bed for clothes and books
as we did. That huge space in front of the TV,
Exercise? Dancing?

You want a small room, not brown either,
You can be dignified in a room like that,
coping admirably, a TV with one remote,
a boudoir chair close by, a room to wrap
around you.

A room like that might have eased
his towering absence from the graduation,
the party afterwards in the sweet darkness.
You stayed too long. You forgot, it's best
to sit alone with a grief like that
and hold its hand.

Dance

Our family had a batch of happiness that autumn.
My brother married in September. Our wedding

was in November, but the October wedding was
my niece's wedding, an old-fashion dance at the

American Legion. All the aunts and uncles
were jolly. The bride led the bunny hop through

the hall, snaking in and out of dancers behind her.
You and my brothers smoked cigars in the corner.

When the bunny hop was over, the music began
again, was it a polka? Not a waltz. You put down

your smoke and reached for my hand, a man
in a hurry to dance with his bride.

Cows

Dusk. After a difficult day,
we walked back through the woods
with our dog, Muffin, the path
littered with fallen tree limbs
and cratered by the hooves
of the neighbors' cows.

We saw them, ahead of us,
young ones, startling
with their big heads,
black and white Holsteins,
bodies firm, not the ponderous
weight of their mothers.

Curious, they came forward.
The dog barked and ran at them,
a show of bravado. They stopped.
I picked Muffin up and held her.

The cows came forward,
big and kindly,
the flutter of their breathing,
a wave of moisture,
in the deepening twilight.

On the Road

Dusk. Slowly darkness turns the snow blue,
the streetlamp, a single light outside my window.

Alone, I've traveled to Stillwater
to observe your birthday, you, born

the day after Christmas above the saloon
where your father tended bar.

I'm paying attention. Not absolute attention
which Simone Weil says is prayer.

You can't call shopping, prayer. Today, I looked
for a gift to mark this trip, the way

you bought me a gift every trip we took.
I bought a paper from the man at the Quik Trip who flirted

with me while talking about the death of his wife.
He thinks we are compatriots and maybe we are.

Otherwise I was alone among the couples and families
masked and polite, wanting a break from the Pandemic.

Back in my room, I raise a toast, not to the family man,
though you were, but the lover, companion, traveler.

I eat my soup, then lower the shades on the darkness
and the old streetlamp, a Christmas star, perfect

for one born above a saloon.

The Life of Plants

A plant which looked to be mature
but then blossomed unexpectedly,
a surge of nutrients from another plant,
cross-fertilization, a noticeable growth.

They flourished, both robust,
sending out shoots for years
until the mate plant weakened,
the source of nutrients changed.

She made up for the loss,
ignoring signs of her own change,
and when the mate plant died,
the ground on which they grew, leveled.

The surviving plant felt the weakness
of her own stems, the stalk not as strong.
She got smaller and smaller,
and finally understood, they were both
just earth, after all.

Mantle

Toward evening
I sat on the side of the bed
looking out at the wide sky,
a mantle over houses,
river, the tree line,
across mountains and oceans,
the same sky.

All the losses, but I thought
of them, not in earth,
though their bones and ashes
are buried there, but
beyond my world,
out there
where eternity stretches.

It lasted a moment.
I said, out loud
God
a big word bigger than sky

God.

Twilight

Photographers call it *sweet light*
The slant of light when the sun
is below the horizon. For painters,
l'heure bleue.

I notice it, the change in the light.
My great tree in the west,
its clumps of dark leaves
like black lace against pale sky
a dress twilight wears.

James Joyce wrote in *Ulysses,*
And my sister played it at the piano,
Just a song at twilight
Love's old sweet song.
Memory sharpest at twilight.

Faces come back if you're quiet.
A yearning for a lover
a soul-longing,
a hymn to the world of things
as they are.

Acknowledgements

I am grateful to the editors and readers of publications and journals where my poems appeared over the years. They are the link in the chain to publication. Thank you.

Artword Quarterly
Boomer Lit
Commonweal
The Dos Passos Review
Dust and Fire
Frontiers: A Journal of Women's Studies
The Grand Gazette
Hamilton Stone Review
Hurricane Alice
J Journal
Lake Street Review
Lalitamba
Lief
Minnesota Monthly
Minnesota Poetry Calendar
Minnesota Voices Competition
Mixed Voices
New Writing for Justice
North Dakota Review
Northern Lit Quarterly
Poetry East
Rock Paper Scissors
Rocked By Waters
Santa Fe Journal
Sidewalks
Sing, Heavenly Muse!
Sleet
St. Paul Almanac
Verve
Water-Stone
Whistling Shade

Blood to Remember: American Poets on the Holocaust
Longing for Home
Mixed Voices
Rocked by the Waters: Poems of Motherhood
Thirty-Three Minnesota Poets
To Sing Along the Way
Wising up Press Anthologies

I am grateful as well to the Minnesota State Arts Board for several grants; the McKnight Foundation for a travel and study grant; the Loft Mentor Series; the Minnesota Humanities Commission.

Thank you to composer Ryan Johnston who set "Evensong" from *Crossing the Waters* to music for voice. Its premier took place in Minneapolis where it was sung at the Source Song Festival.

These are friends and colleagues who have sustained me as a writer over the years: Sharon Chmielarz, Deborah Keenan, Jim Moore, Monica Ochtrup, Sheila O'Connor, the late Alvaro Cardona-Hine, and the late Jim White. In the beginning, I was a member of the writing group Onionskin and stayed for a dozen years, learning my craft with those talented and generous writers.

Thanks to John Toren, for book design and the photograph on the cover. Thanks to my friend, Zoe St. Mane, for the author photograph taken at Hawk Ridge.

My late husband, Eugene Jax, was the truest of friends to the poet and my first reader. Thank you.

About the Author

Norita Dittberner-Jax was born and raised in the Frogtown neighborhood of Saint Paul, the sixth of seven children. She was educated in parochial schools and graduated from the (then) College of Saint Catherine. She started writing when her children were young, just as the Twin Cities area was becoming a center for creative writing with the emergence of the Loft. She taught English in the public schools of Saint Paul, and creative writing for the Writers-in-the Schools Program and at the Perpich Center for the Arts. Her second marriage, to Eugene Jax, brought international travel and a great interest in art. In retirement from teaching, she returned to academic life, earning an MFA in poetry from Hamline University. Norita is one of the poetry editors for Red Bird Chapbooks.